Devious Chess
How to bend the rules and win

Amatzia Avni

BATSFORD

First published in the United Kingdom in 2006 by

B T Batsford
151 Freston Road
London
W10 6TH

An imprint of Anova Books Company Ltd

ISBN 0713490047

ISBN (13) 9780713490046

A CIP catalogue record for this book is available from the British Library.
10 9 8 7 6 5 4 3 2 1

Cover reproduction by Classic Scan Pte Ltd, Singapore

Printed and bound by MPG Books Ltd, Bodmin, Cornwall

This book can be ordered direct from the publisher at the website:
www.anovabooks.com

Or try your local bookshop

Contents

Acknowledgements

As usual, my old friend **Raaphy Persitz** was of immense help, making the text clearer and more reader-friendly. GM **Alon Greenfeld** assisted in solving the mystery of some tricky and complicated positions. I extend my gratitude to both of them.

The book is dedicated with love to my wife and children—**Naama, Yuval, Ohad** and **Yael.**

Introduction

We live in an age where many people are bored with their lives and are looking for change. Some desire to live in another country; others yearn to change their workplace; there are those who would gladly adopt another family or be adopted by one. A poem by the Israeli Yona Wallach expresses the hope that there might exist another kind of sex...

In short, people are averse to routine and search feverishly elsewhere, towards anything or anyone who will inject some excitement into their world.

I wonder: Is there a *'different'* kind of chess?

The game of kings has been deeply explored, in each of its phases, for centuries. In the last two decades, computer software has unravelled many of its secrets.

The vast majority of modern games follow well-trodden paths. In a sense, they are all variations on a theme: fresh nuances, intriguing subtleties... but basically, leafing through chess journals, a seasoned player is likely to observe repeated, familiar patterns.

The game below is a typical sample of such a performance.

Nikolaidis – Marciano
NAO chess club championship,
France 2004

1 d4 ♘f6 2 c4 e6 3 ♘f3 d5 4 ♗g5 ♗e7 5 e3 0-0 6 ♘c3 h6 7 ♗h4 ♘e4 8 ♗xe7 ♕xe7 9 ♖c1 ♘xc3 10 ♖xc3 c6 11 ♕b3 ♘d7 12 ♕a3 ♕xa3 13 ♖xa3 ♖d8 14 c5 ♖e8 15 b4 e5 16 ♗e2 exd4 17 ♘xd4 ♘f8 18 ♔d2 ♘e6 19 ♗d3 ♗d7 20 ♖c1 ♔f8 21 ♖b3 ♘xd4 22 exd4 b5

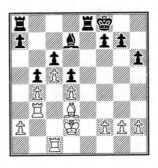

23 ♖a3 a5 24 ♖xa5 ♖xa5 25 bxa5 ♖a8 26 a4 bxa4 27 a6 ♗c8 28 ♖a1 ♗xa6 29 ♖xa4 ♗b7 30 ♖xa8+ ♗xa8 31 ♗a6

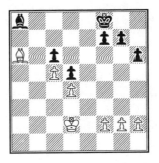

31...♔e7 32 ♔e3 ♔f6 33 h4 ♔f5 34 ♗c8+ ♔g6 35 ♔f4 ♔f6 36 h5 ♔e7 37 ♔f5 ♔d8 38 ♗a6 ♔c7 39 ♔e5 ♔d7 40 g4 ♔e7 41 ♔f5 f6 42 ♗c8 ♔f7 43 f3 ♔e7 44 ♔g6 ♔f8 45 f4 ♔g8 46 g5 hxg5 47 fxg5 fxg5 48 ♔xg5 ♔f8 49 ♔g6 ♔g8 50 h6 gxh6 51 ♔xh6 ♔f7 52 ♔g5 ♔e7 53 ♔f5 ♔d8 54 ♗a6 ♔e7 55 ♔e5 ♔d7 56 ♔f6 ♔d8 57 ♔e6 ♔c7 58 ♔e7 ♔b8 59 ♔d7 ♔a7 60 ♗c8 ♔b8 61 ♔d8 ♔a7 62 ♔c7 ♗b7 63 ♗d7 ♗a6 1-0

A clear-cut, convincing example of positional strangulation. Without detracting from White's fine technique, one must acknowledge that the whole game revolves around well-known motifs. 7...♘e4 is a familiar *freeing device*, exchanging pieces to *simplify* the position. Soon afterwards White commences a *minority attack* on the queenside. He gains *space* and tries *to create a passed pawn*. The pawn structure guarantees White the better endgame and when, following 31 ♗a6, *the black bishop is incarcerated* on a8, the end is near.

Thereafter White *infiltrates* his opponent's formation with his king, using *zugzwang*. When Black's stalemate trick fails, he throws in the towel.

If the previous game was of a distinctive strategic type, tactical battles also rest heavily upon familiar themes.

Naiditsch – Zeller
German championship 2002

1 e4 c5 2 ♘f3 e6 3 d4 cxd4 4 ♘xd4 a6 5 ♗d3 ♗c5 6 ♘b3 ♗e7 7 0-0 d6 8 c4 ♘f6 9 ♘c3 b6 10 f4 ♘bd7 11 ♕f3 ♗b7 12 ♔h1 ♕c7 13 ♗d2 h5 14 ♕h3 ♘g4 15 ♖ac1 ♘df6 16 f5 ♕d7 17 ♘d4 ♖c8 18 b3 ♗d8 19 fxe6 fxe6 20 ♘d5! 0-0

Accepting the gift with 20...exd5 21 exd5 0-0 22 ♗f5 is unappetizing.

21 ♘xf6+ ♗xf6 22 ♕xh5 ♘e5 23 ♗b1 ♖c5 24 ♕h3 ♗c8 25 ♘e2 b5 26 ♗e3 ♖c6 27 ♘f4 bxc4?

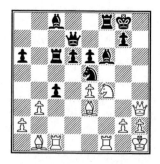

28 ♘g6!! ♔xg6 29 e5 ♘xe5 30 ♕h7+ ♔f7 31 ♖xf6+ ♔xf6 32 ♖f1+ ♔e7 33 ♕xg7+ ♘f7 34 ♖xf7+! ♖xf7 35 ♗g5+ ♔e8 36 ♕g8+ 1-0

A bright attacking tussle, but again there is nothing new under the sun. The advance f2-f4-f5 is designed *to open an important file*; the ♘d5 *positional sacrifice* in the Sicilian has been played in many similar positions; 28 ♘g6 demonstrates *deflection of a blockader*; once the ♘e5 is out of the way, White *opens a critical diagonal* (29 e5!). The two exchange sacrifices *demolish the defenders* and pave the way for the queen to complete the task against the bare monarch.

The present work focuses on *a different kind of chess*. In the absence of a commonly accepted terminology, we'll describe it as *'devious chess'* or *'unconventional chess'*. By these expressions – which we shall use interchangeably – we have in mind a kind of play that contains several characteristics from the following list:

❖ sailing in uncharted waters

❖ lacking familiar anchors and stratagems

❖ complex

❖ risky

❖ opportunistic

❖ impudent

❖ not obvious

❖ double-edged

❖ materially unbalanced

❖ sometimes unsound

Aside from the pleasure and excitement 'devious chess' imparts to its adherent, it is a source of trouble for the opponent and quite tough to fight against. Even software programs, when confronted on uncharted territory, drop in their playing strength; let alone human beings, who frequently lose their equanimity when thrown into alien surroundings.

Going through the following game, readers will immediately feel that it is different, in a fundamental way, from the chess they are accustomed to.

Sorokin – Riumin
Soviet championship, Moscow 1931

1 d4 ♘f6 2 ♘f3 e6 3 e3 c5 4 ♗d3 ♘c6 5 c3 ♕c7 6 ♘bd2 b6 7 ♕e2 cxd4 8 exd4 ♘d5 9 g3 ♗e7 10 ♘c4 ♗b7 11 0-0 h5

Until now the game has developed along 'normal' channels. With his last move Black makes a bold attempt to initiate a direct attack.

12 ♗e4 ♘f6 13 ♗f4 d6 14 ♘g5

Black is not the only side with evil intentions; 15 ♗g6 and 15 d5 are now potential white threats.

14...♘xe4 15 ♘xe4 0-0-0 16 a4 g5?!

16...e5 is natural and good, but Black has other ideas.

17 ♘xg5 e5 18 dxe5 ♘xe5 19 ♗xe5 dxe5 20 ♘xf7 ♕c6

It appears as if Black has conjured up a dangerous initiative. However, White can parry this burst of action and retain his material advantage.

21 f3 ♗c5+ 22 ♔g2 h4

22...e4 23 fxe4 (23 f4 e3+ 24 ♖f3 h4 is less clear) ♕xe4+ 24 ♕xe4 ♗xe4+ 25 ♔h3 is insufficient.

23 ♘xd8 h3+ 24 ♔h1 ♖xd8

Black needs only one more move – 25...e4! – to gain success; but it is White's turn.

25 b4

25...e4

As 25...♗e7 26 ♘xe5 is tantamount to capitulation, Black abandons material considerations in search of some practical chances.

26 bxc5 ♕xc5

If 26...exf3 27 ♕f2 ♕xc5? 28 ♕xc5+ and there is no time for 28...f2+.

After the text move, a very peculiar situation arises. A rook ahead, it seems that any sensible move wins for White. As a matter of fact – while he does have several promising lines at his disposal on each turn – White must also take certain care. It is not as simple as it looks.

27 ♘d2

The pin in the variation 27 fxe4 ♖e8 28 ♖f4 is easier to handle than the line which occurs now.

27...exf3 28 ♘xf3 ♖f8

Threatening 28...♕f5(h5).

29 ♖f2

Now what? Black's resources seem to have dried up.

29...a5

Incredible. Black creates a haven for his king on a7, ostensibly giving

White a free hand in converting his huge material superiority.

30 ♖d1?! ♔b8

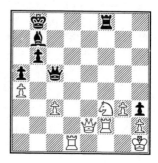

Let us imagine what is going on in White's mind: he knows that his position is winning; he is frustrated by his opponent dragging on the game. Yet a clear-cut victory is not to hand. An eventual ♔h1-g1 would only transform one pin into another.

31 ♖e1 ♔a7 32 ♕e3 ♖e8!

Inviting 33 ♕xc5 ♖xe1+ or 33 ♕xe8 ♕xf2 which both lose for White.

33 ♕d2 ♖d8 34 ♕e2 ♖d3!

Tricks, tricks, and more tricks. How should White disentangle?

35 c4 ♕d4!

Politely rejecting 35...♕xf2? 36 ♕xf2 ♖xf3, which regains some material but transposes into a lost ending.

36 ♕f1 ♗c6 37 ♖e7+

"Even at this point White had excellent chances – by pushing his g-pawn" – Soltis. [1] One sample variation supporting this assessment is 37 g4 ♖xf3!? 38 ♖xf3 ♕f4 39 ♕xh3 ♗xf3+ 40 ♔g1 ♕d4+ 41 ♔f1, when White comes out on top.

37...♔b8 38 ♖e8+ ♔a7 39 ♖e7+ ♔b8

Black had indulged in all sort of tactical traps; then, with some apparently passive moves (29...a5, 30...♔b8, 36...♗c6) he dared White to make headway. Poor Sorokin finds himself in an unenviable state and at the end he cracks under the pressure.

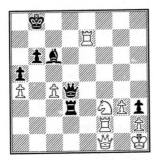

40 g4?

This is definitely the wrong time for this push.

40...♖xf3! 41 ♖e8+

41 ♖xf3 ♗xf3+ 42 ♕xf3 ♕a1+ mating.

41...♔a7 42 ♖e7+ ♔a6 43 c5+ ♖d3+ 44 ♔g1 ♕xg4+ 45 ♖g2 ♕xg2+ 46 ♕xg2 hxg2 0-1

* * * *

The Sorokin – Riumin game is an apt illustration of 'devious chess'; a concept that we are going to develop and explore in the ensuing chapters.

My first ever book, *Creative Chess* (Cadogan 1991, 1997), was about new ideas, concentrating on innovative and original play. *Devious Chess* is a natural sequel: similarly advocating stepping aside from the main road, it is focused on a different approach, a change of attitude.

We invite you to join us on a journey to a fascinating, out-of-the-ordinary type of game. Readers will be enriched; hopefully some of them will dare to give this form of play a try themselves!

Part One:

The Nature of 'Devious Chess'

The following chapters demonstrate the various aspects of 'devious chess'. In order to flourish, it needs unexplored territory so that a player will be able to shun familiar rules, structures and stratagems. The opening chapter presents a sample of such surroundings.

Next we are introduced to the complexity side of this 'different' type of chess. Chapter 2 exhibits some extraordinary positions where tension reaches enormous heights; a lot of pieces hang and the number of plausible alternatives increases beyond human capabilities.

'Devious' chess is not always sound. The style of 'coffeehouse chess' is the topic of chapter 3. It affords a lot of fun and good practical chances, even if 'Fritz' frowns.

Chapter 4 discusses surprising, shrewd and non-obvious aspects of unconventional chess.

To conclude this part, in chapter 5 the reader is acquainted with special moves which are more common in 'devious chess' than in an ordinary, conventional game. Some of these moves are deceptive in appearance; others are noteworthy for their destructive effect.

Chapter One:

Virgin Soil

A prominent characteristic of 'devious chess' is to seek new, hitherto unexplored lands. Avoiding well-trodden paths from the very first moves often leads to juicy, freakish positions. There are more chances of finding (chess) life in far-away uninhabited jungles than in nearby metropolitan environments.

K. Grigorian – Gulko

USSR 1975

1 d4 ♘f6 2 c4 e6 3 ♘c3 ♗b4 4 ♕c2 d5 5 a3 ♗xc3+ 6 ♕xc3 ♘e4 7 ♕c2 c5 8 dxc5 ♘c6 9 cxd5 exd5 10 ♘f3 ♗f5 11 b4 0-0

Rejecting the dangerous invitation to enter the line 11...♘g3 12 ♕b2 ♘xh1 13 ♕xg7.

12 ♗b2 b6

Again, 12...♘g3 13 ♕c3 d4 14 ♘xd4 ♘xd4 15 fxg3 is in White's favour.

13 b5 bxc5 14 bxc6 ♕a5+ 15 ♘d2 ♖ab8 16 ♖d1 d4 17 c7 ♕xc7 18 ♘xe4

18 ♗xd4!

18...♗xe4 19 ♕d2 ♖fe8

In return for the sacrificed piece, Black has achieved a dominating position. White tries to extricate himself by returning material.

20 h4 ♖b6 21 ♖h3 ♕b7 22 ♗xd4 cxd4 23 ♕xd4 ♗c2

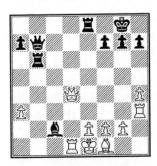

24 ♖e3 ♖f8 25 ♖a1 ♖b1+ 26 ♔d2 ♗g6 27 h5 ♗xh5 28 ♖e5 ♗g6 29 ♖c5 ♖b8 30 ♖c1 ♖b3 31 ♔e1

This 'normal' position has been reached through the strangest of means: notice ...♖f8-e8-f8, ♖a1-d1-a1, ♔e1-d2-e1.

31...♕e7 32 ♕c5 ♕xc5 33 ♖xc5 ♖b1+ 34 ♖c1 ♖xa1 35 ♖xa1

Glancing at this peaceful position, it is hard to believe that ♖a1 is in fact White's *king's* rook, arriving at its destination via h3-e3-e5-c5-c1!

35...♔f8 36 ♔d2 ♖b3 37 g4 ♔e7 38 ♗g2 ♔d6 39 f4 f6 40 a4 a5 41 ♖c1 ♖b2+ 42 ♔e3 ♗c2 43 ♖h1 ♗xa4 44 ♖xh7 ♗d1 45 ♗f3 a4 46 ♖xg7 a3 47 ♖a7 a2 48 ♔d4 ½-½

Miles – Vaisser

Olympiad, Elista 1998

1 d4 e6 2 ♘f3 f5 3 d5!? exd5 4 ♕xd5 d6 5 ♘g5 ♕e7 6 ♘xh7

Winning a pawn at the cost of a lag in development.

6...c6 7 ♕b3 ♖xh7

If 7...♗e6 then 8 ♕g3, when 8...♖xh7 is countered by 9 ♕g6+.

8 ♕xg8 ♖h4 9 ♕b3 ♘a6 10 ♕e3 ♖e4 11 ♕d2 ♘b4 12 ♕d1

This is the queen's seventh move within the first 12 moves. 12 ♘c3? fails to 12...♖d4.

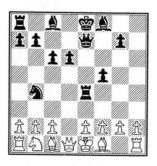

12...♖d4 13 ♘d2 f4 14 a3

Black was threatening 14...♗f5. 14 c3 is of course a gross blunder, allowing mate in one.

14...♘d5 15 c3 ♘e3! 16 fxe3 ♕h4+ 17 g3 fxg3 18 ♗g2 gxh2+

18...♗h3 is tempting but 19 cxd4 ♗xg2 20 ♘f3! ♗xf3 21 exf3 g2+ 22 ♔e2 gxh1=♕ 23 ♕xh1 cedes White an extra pawn (Miles).

19 ♔f1 ♕f6+ 20 ♔e1 ♕h4+ 21 ♔f1 ½-½

Borisenko – Dorfman

USSR 1975

1 d4 d5 2 c4 dxc4 3 ♘f3 ♘d7 4 ♘bd2 b5 5 b3?! c3 6 ♘b1 b4 7 a3 c5 8 dxc5 ♘xc5 9 ♕c2 ♗e6 10 e3 a5

Not 10...♗(♘)xb3? 11 ♗b5+.

11 ♗b5+ ♗d7 12 ♗xd7+ ♕xd7 13 axb4 ♘d3+ 14 ♔f1 ♘xb4 15 ♕xc3 ♖c8 16 ♕d2 ♕d3+! 17 ♔g1

17 ♕xd3? ♖xc1+.

17...♕xb3

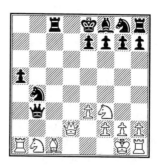

Total underdevelopment.

18 ♘d4 ♕d3 19 ♕xd3 ♘xd3 20 ♗d2 ♘f6 21 f3 e5 22 ♘b3 ♗b4

22...a4 is even better, as 23 ♖xa4? loses to 23...♖b8.

23 ♔f1 0-0 24 ♔e2 ♖fd8 25 ♘xa5

White regains his pawn, but his position lacks harmony and soon collapses against Black's organized army.

25...e4 26 ♘b3 ♗xd2 27 ♘1xd2 ♘d5 28 ♘xe4 ♖c2+ 29 ♘bd2

29 ♔xd3? ♘b4 mate. 29 ♘ed2 is considerably more stubborn.

29...f5 30 ♘g3

Another possibility is 30 ♔xd3 ♘b4++ 31 ♔e2 fxe4 32 ♖hd1 exf3+ 33 gxf3 ♘a2!.

30...♘c3+ 31 ♔f1 ♖xd2 0-1

Charlov – Voulin

St. Petersburg 1998

1 e4 c5 2 ♘c3 ♘c6 3 ♘f3 ♘d4 4 ♗c4 ♘xf3+ 5 gxf3 a6 6 d4 b5 7 ♗d5 ♖a7 8 ♗f4

White appears to be active: 6...b5 looks suspect at this early stage. Yet it is Black who will dictate matters from now on.

8...e6! 9 ♗b8 ♖c7 10 ♗a8

An outlandish move but after 10 ♗xc7 ♕xc7, the ♗d5 is lost.

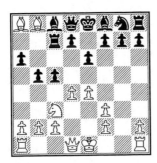

10...cxd4 11 ♗xc7

Or 11 ♕xd4 ♖c4 12 ♕e3 (12 ♕d3 ♕b6) ♗c5.

11...♕xc7 12 ♕xd4 ♕b8 13 ♗d5 b4! 14 ♘a4 exd5 15 exd5 ♗d6 16 0-0-0 ♘e7 17 ♕xg7 ♗e5 18 ♕g4 d6 19 ♕c4 0-0 20 f4 ♗f6 21 b3 a5 22 ♖he1 ♗f5 23 ♖e2 ♘g6 24 ♖g1 ♔h8 25 ♖d2 ♖e8 26 f3 ♕a7 27 ♖gd1 ♕e3 28 ♕a6 ♘xf4 0-1

Reckless gambit-type of play often poses insurmountable problems for our adversary.

Byrk – Litvinov

USSR 1970

1 c4 ♘f6 2 ♘c3 g6 3 d4 d5 4 ♗f4 ♗g7 5 e3 0-0 6 ♘f3 ♗g4 7 ♕b3 ♗xf3 8 gxf3 c5 9 ♕xb7 ♘bd7 10 dxc5 d4 11 exd4 e5 12 ♗xe5? ♘xe5 13 dxe5 ♖b8 14 ♕xa7

After 14 moves, White is five pawns ahead (!). 'Fritz' assesses White as clearly better, under-estimating his lag in development.

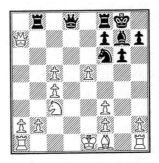

14...♘h5 15 ♘d5 ♗xe5 16 ♘e7+? ♔h8 17 ♖d1

17 ♘c6 ♕e8.

17...♗d4 18 ♗e2 ♖e8 19 c6?

An error, but 19 ♘c6 ♖xb2! is also unsavoury: 20 ♘xd8? allows mate, while 20 ♘xd4 ♘f4 or 20 0-0 ♕g5+ 21 ♔h1 ♗xc5 offers no joy.

19...♗xa7 20 ♖xd8 ♖bxd8 21 c7 ♖a8 22 c8=♕ ♖axc8 23 ♘xc8 ♖xc8 24 ♖g1 ♘f4 25 ♖g4 g5 26 ♗f1 f6 27 h4 h5 28 ♖g1 ♖e8+ 29 ♔d2 ♗xf2 30 ♖h1 g4 31 fxg4 hxg4 32 c5 ♗xc5 33 ♔c3 g3 34 ♔c4 ♗f2 35 b4 ♖e1 0-1

It is not only in the opening phase that players may wish to deviate towards the unknown; unexplored islands can be found also in middlegames, as the next three examples demonstrate.

Tal – Panno

Interzonal, Portoroz 1958

1 e4 e5 2 ♘f3 ♘c6 3 ♗b5 a6 4 ♗a4 ♘f6 5 0-0 ♗e7 6 ♖e1 b5 7 ♗b3 d6 8 c3 0-0 9 h3 ♘d7 10 d4 ♘b6 11 ♗e3 exd4 12 cxd4 ♘a5 13 ♗c2 c5

A standard Ruy Lopez position. However, Tal now navigates the game towards sharp, uncharted waters.

14 e5!? dxe5 15 ♘xe5 ♘bc4 16 ♕d3 f5 17 ♗b3 f4 18 ♗d2 ♘xb3 19 ♘c6!?

The sane 19 ♕xb3 ♕d5 is better for Black; so White heads for an unbalanced, fantastic position, illustrated in the following diagram.

19...♘xa1 20 ♘xd8 ♗f5 21 ♕f3 ♖axd8 22 ♖xe7 ♗xb1

23 ♗xf4 ♖xd4 24 ♕g4! ♗g6 25 ♕e6+ ♗f7 26 ♕f5 ♘c2 27 b3 ♗g6?

27...♖d1+ 28 ♔h2 ♘d2! 29 ♗xd2 (29 ♕xc2? ♘f1+ 30 ♔g1 ♘e3+) ♖xd2 is correct, when Black holds the edge.

28 ♖xg7+! ♔xg7 29 ♗h6+ ♔xh6 30 ♕xf8+ ♔g5 31 bxc4 bxc4 32 g3 ♗e4 33 h4+ ♔g4 34 ♔h2 ♗f5 35 ♕f6! h6 36 ♕e5 ♖e4 37 ♕g7+ ♔f3

38 ♕c3+ ♘e3

38...♔xf2 39 ♕xc2+ ♔f1 is about equal.

39 ♔g1 ♗g4 40 fxe3 h5 41 ♕e1 ♖xe3?

A decisive mistake. 41...♖e6! still keeps the balance.

42 ♕f1+ ♔e4 43 ♕xc4+ ♔f3 44 ♕f1+ ♔e4 45 ♕xa6 ♔d4 46 ♕d6+ ♔c4 47 a4 ♖e1+ 48 ♔f2 ♖e2+ 49 ♔f1 ♖a2 50 ♕a6+ ♔d4 51 a5

White comes first in the mutual pawn-race.

51...c4 52 ♕b6+ ♔d5 53 a6 ♖a1+ 54 ♔f2 c3 55 a7 c2 56 ♕b3+ ♔d6 57 ♕d3+ 1-0

After 57...♔e6 (best) 58 ♕xc2 ♖xa7 59 ♕e4+!, the rook falls.

A fabulous fight, in which, it seems, both players sought victory at all costs.

Reshko – Faibisovich

Leningrad 1969

1 c4 g6 2 ♘c3 c5 3 g3 ♗g7 4 ♗g2 ♘c6 5 e4 d6 6 d3 ♘f6 7 ♘ge2 0-0 8 0-0 a6 9 h3 ♖b8 10 f4 ♘e8 11 ♗e3 ♘d4 12 ♕d2 b5 13 ♖ae1 b4 14 ♘d1 b3 15 ♗xd4 bxa2

Following a mundane opening system, play now explodes:

16 ♗xg7! a1=♕ 17 ♗c3!

The newborn queen is temporarily out of play, while opening lines and diagonals on the kingside is imminent.

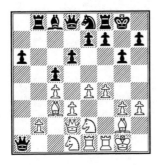

17...♕a4 18 f5 f6 19 ♕h6 e5 20 fxe6 e.p. ♗xe6 21 ♘f4 ♗f7

21...♘g7? 22 ♕xg7+ ♔xg7 23 ♘xe6+ is in White's favour, while on 21...♕ad7 22 ♘xe6 ♕xe6, 23 e5 (threatening 24 ♗d5) is powerful.

22 ♘e3 ♕ad7?

Here the immediate 22...♖b3!, intending to remove the menacing bishop with 23...♖xc3, is indicated.

23 ♘g4 ♖b3

Too late.

24 ♘h5! ♗e6 25 ♖xf6! ♕de7

Black resigned, in view of 26 ♖xg6+.

Planinc – Baretic

Cateske Toplice 1968

1 e4 e6 2 d4 d5 3 ♘c3 ♗b4 4 e5 c5 5 a3 ♗xc3+ 6 bxc3 ♘e7 7 ♕g4 ♕c7 8 ♕xg7 ♖g8 9 ♕xh7 cxd4 10 ♔d1

Over the years this strange system had become main line theory.

10...♘bc6 11 ♘f3 dxc3 12 ♘g5 ♖f8 13 f4 ♗d7 14 ♖b1 ♘a5 15 ♗d3 ♕c5 16 ♕h3 ♗c6 17 ♘h7 0-0-0 18 ♘xf8 ♖xf8

White has won the exchange and in any type of ending this factor, plus his passed h-pawn, should suffice. But first he must withstand Black's initiative in the middlegame.

19 ♕e3 d4 20 ♕e2 ♘f5 21 ♖f1 ♖d8 22 ♖b4 a6 23 ♔e1 ♘e3 24 ♖g1?! ♘d5 25 ♖b1 ♘c4 26 h4 ♘xa3 27 ♖a1 ♘c4

White is reluctant to exchange his dark-squared bishop for this knight (24 ♗xe3, 27 ♗xa3) but the knight pair is a nuisance: 28 ♗xc4? d3.

28 h5 ♘b2 29 h6 ♗b5 30 ♖h1 ♗xd3 31 cxd3 ♘b4 32 h7 ♘2xd3+ 33 ♔f1 ♘xc1 34 ♕g4?

34 ♖xc1 d3 35 ♕d2! is considerably better.

34...♘c2 35 ♕g8 ♘xa1 36 h8=♕

A striking position.

36...♖xg8 37 ♕xg8+ ♔c7 38 ♕xf7+ ♔b6 39 ♕xe6+ ♔a5 40 g4 d3 41 ♕d7 ♕e3 42 ♕c7+ ♔a4 43 ♕c4+ ♔a3 44 ♔g2 d2 45 e6 ♘c2 0-1

Lastly, it is feasible to find places where no man has ever trodden, even in few-pieces endgames.

Topalov – Morozevich

Madrid 1996

White to play

In a mutual pawn race, sophistic-ation is seldom required: he who comes (promotes) first, wins – is a simple rule of thumb. There are exceptions, though.

51 ♖g2+ ♔b1 52 g6 b3 53 h5 b2 54 ♖a3!

Black is ahead in the race but now some strange things happen. First of all, a liquidation on the queenside – as, for example, after 54...a1=♕? 55 ♖g1+, leaves Black helpless against the g and h-pawn pair. By the same token, 54...♔a1 55 ♖xc3 b1=♕ 56 ♖cc2 is unclear, despite Black's huge material advantage. A similar variation occurs in the game:

54...♖d8 55 ♖xc3 a1=♕ 56 ♖b3 ♕a6 57 ♖bxb2+ ♔c1 58 ♖a2!

Such positions are rarely encountered outside the realm of chess composition.

58...♕e6+ 59 ♔h2 ♔b1 60 ♖ab2+ ♔c1 61 ♖a2 ♔b1 62 ♖af2! ♔c1

Neither is 62...♖d1 63 g7 ♕g8 64 ♖f8 much good.

63 g7 ♕g8 64 ♖f1+ ♖d1 65 ♖xd1+ ♔xd1 66 h6 ♔e1 67 ♔g1 ♕b3

Else 68 h7 decides.

68 g8=♕ ♕xe3+ 69 ♔h1 ♕xh6+ 70 ♖h2 1-0

Dvoiris – Svidler

Russian championship, Elista 1997

White to play

White is behind in material, and this factor, combined with the insecure position of his king, suggests that his days are numbered.

41 ♕xd4 ♖xd4 is hopeless, so White tries something else.

41 ♕e7 ♖b8 42 ♕b4 ♗d5+ 43 ♘xd5 ♖xb4 44 axb4

With the black king locked in the corner, this unusual ending is not trivial. First of all, Black proceeds to increase his material gains.

44...♕c4+ 45 ♔b2 h5 46 g3 ♕g4 47 ♘f4 ♕xg3 48 ♘xh5 ♕e5+ 49 ♔b3 ♕xh5 50 c3

A position not to be found in textbooks. Black is well aware that without the assistance of his king, victory is impossible. Hence the winning idea is zugzwang.

50...♕e2 51 ♗c4 ♕d1+ 52 ♔b2 ♕d2+ 53 ♔b3 ♕c1 54 ♗f7 ♕b1+ 55 ♔c4

Or 55 ♔a3 ♕c2 56 c4 ♕c3+ 57 ♔a4 ♕b2 58 c5 ♕e2 59 ♔b3 ♕d3+ 60 ♔b2 ♕b5 61 ♔c3 a5, when Black attains a similar position to the game.

55...♕c2 56 ♔d4 ♕e2! 57 c4 ♕b2+ 58 ♔c5 ♕a3 59 ♔b6

Black intended 59...a5.

59...♕xb4+ 60 ♔xa6 ♕c5

After a long journey, a familiar pattern is achieved: the queen will stalk the enemy king from the distance of a knight's move, until lack of moves will force the white bishop to withdraw from its post.

61 ♔b7 ♕d6 62 ♔c8 ♕e7 0-1

In view of 63 ♔b8 ♕d7 64 ♔a8 ♕c7 65 ♗d5 ♕d6 66 ♗f7 ♕b6 etc.

Chapter Two:

Raising the Tension

The level of tension in a chess game oscillates constantly. *[We use the word 'tension' to define a position, not to describe a psychological state of mind].* At times the game unwinds at a leisurely pace; at other times it soars to boiling point.

'Devious chess' witnesses a frequent rise in tension, as it is characterized by sharp positions and constant walking on the edge. We will look at typical situations where high tension occurs.

Hanging Pieces

Circumstances where pieces are 'hanging' are quite baffling. When one piece can be captured in several ways, or several pieces are *en prise* simultaneously, the thick forest of viable candidate moves is difficult to handle.

Y. Geller – E. Kogan

Odessa team championship 1946

1 e4 c5 2 ♘f3 d6 3 d4 cxd4 4 ♕xd4 ♘c6 5 ♗b5 ♗d7 6 ♗xc6 ♗xc6 7 ♘c3 ♘f6 8 ♗g5 e6 9 0-0

Nowadays, queenside castling is more common.

9...♗e7 10 ♖ad1 0-0 11 ♖fe1 ♕c7 12 h3 b5 13 ♘h2 ♖fd8 14 ♖d3 a5 15 ♖f3 b4

Black has developed sensibly and it is difficult to assess the chances of White's impending onslaught.

16 ♖xf6!? bxc3 17 ♘g4 h5

17...gxf6 18 ♘xf6+ ♔h8 19 ♕xc3 is unattractive, so Black attacks another white piece. With two of his pieces threatened, Geller, a fearless tactician already in his youth, responds with yet another sacrifice.

18 ♗h6!

Intending to counter 18...hxg4 by 19 ♖g6! e5 20 ♖xg7+ ♔h8 21 ♕c4 with a strong initiative.

18...e5

No fewer than four white pieces are now threatened.

19 ♕e3 hxg4

19...gxf6 20 ♕f3!.

20 ♗xg7 ♔xg7?

With so many alternatives at his disposal, Black cannot sustain the pressure. As Geller points out, [2] 20...♗xf6 21 ♗xf6 ♔f8! 22 ♕g5 cxb2 would force White to accept a peaceful conclusion: 23 ♕g7+ ♔e8 24 ♕g8+ ♔d7 25 ♕xg4+ with perpetual check.

21 ♕h6+ ♔g8 22 ♖f5 ♗e8 23 ♖h5 f6 24 ♖h4 ♕c8 25 ♕h8+ ♔f7 26 ♖h7+ ♔e6 27 ♕g7 ♔d7 28 ♖e3 cxb2 29 ♕xe7+ ♔c6 30 ♖c3+ ♔b6 31 ♖xc8 b1=♕+ 32 ♔h2 ♖d7 33 ♕xe8 ♖xh7 34 ♕c6+ 1-0

Jonathan – Blumenfeld

Tel-Aviv championship 1958

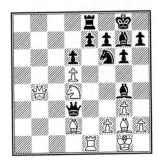

White to play

26 ♗f1

The black queen lacks flight squares but Black has prepared for this:

26...♘xd5

Ready to counter 27 ♗xd3 with 27...♘xb4 28 ♗xb4 ♗xd4 29 ♖e4 e5 30 ♖xg4 d5! which leads to an unclear position; and 27 ♕a4 with 27...♕xd2 28 ♕xe8+ ♗f8.

27 ♖xe7!

Adding fuel to the fire, a common attribute of unconventional chess. The rook is taboo (27...♘xe7 28 ♗xd3; 27...♖xe7 28 ♕b8+). So the ♖e8 has to move, but where to?

27...♖a8?

27...♖c8 or 27...♖f8 is correct, when the result would be in doubt. The text move succumbs to White's next shot.

28 ♕a5!!

Once again White places a piece on an unprotected square. This time there is no remedy.

28...♖xa5 29 ♖e8+ ♗f8 30 ♗h6 ♕xf1+ 31 ♔xf1 ♗h3+ 32 ♔e1 1-0

S. Bernstein – Cass

Marshall chess club championship 1939

1 e4 c5 2 ♘f3 e6 3 d4 cxd4 4 ♘xd4 ♘f6 5 ♘c3 ♗b4 6 e5 ♘d5 7 ♕g4 ♘xc3

Modern alternatives are 7...0-0 8 ♗h6 g6 9 ♗xf8 ♕xf8; 7...g6; or 7...♔f8.

8 ♕xg7 ♖f8 9 a3 ♗a5 10 b4 ♗c7 11 ♗g5 ♗xe5 12 ♕xe5 f6 13 ♘f5!!

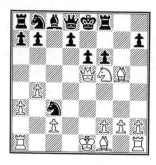

13...♘d5

13...fxg5 (13...fxe5? 14 ♘d6 mate) loses to 14 ♘d6+ ♚e7 15 ♕xg5+, as 15...♚xd6 allows 16 ♕c5 mate. 13...♘c6 is the lesser evil.

14 ♗e2! ♘c6 15 ♗h5+ ♖f7 16 ♕e4 ♕c7 17 ♘h6 ♘d8 18 ♘xf7 ♘xf7 19 ♗g6+ ♚xf7 20 ♕xh7+ ♚e8 21 ♕g6+ ♚e7 22 ♗xf6+ ♘xf6 23 ♕g7+ 1-0

E. Vladimirov – V. Mikhalevski

Calcutta 2001

1 d4 ♘f6 2 c4 c5 3 d5 b5 4 cxb5 a6 5 b6 e6 6 ♘c3 ♘xd5 7 ♘xd5 exd5 8 ♕xd5 ♘c6 9 ♘f3 ♖b8 10 ♗d2 ♗e7 11 ♗c3 0-0 12 e4 ♖xb6 13 ♗c4 ♘b4 14 ♕d2 ♗b7 15 a3 d5 16 exd5 ♘xd5 17 ♗e5 ♖g6 18 0-0-0 ♘b6 19 ♗xf7+! ♚xf7 20 ♕f4+ ♚e6

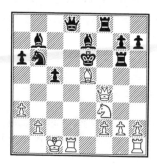

A wild position where both queens are hanging. 21 ♖xd8 ♖xf4 or 21 ♕e3 ♘d5 achieve nothing, but White has a more attractive continuation:

21 ♗f6!!

The bishop may be captured in four ways. [Incidentally, this is not a record; Ponomariov – Garcia Ilundain, Pampelona 1996-97, saw 1 e4 d5 2 exd5 ♕xd5 3 ♘c3 ♕d8 4 d4 ♘f6 5 ♘f3 c6 6 ♗c4 ♗f5 7 ♘e5 e6 8 g4 ♗g6 9 h4 ♗b4 10 ♖h3 ♘bd7 11 ♕e2 ♘b6 12 h5 ♗e4 13 ♗f4 ♕xd4 14 ♖d1 ♗d3. After Black's last move White can eliminate the ♗d3 in six different ways!

The remainder of this fascinating game was 15 ♖hxd3 ♕xf4 16 ♖d4 ♕h2 17 ♘xf7 0-0 18 ♗xe6 ♘bd5 19 ♕e5 ♕g2 20 ♖xb4 ♘xb4 21 ♖d8 ♘xc2+ 22 ♚e2 ♕g1? (22...♖axd8 23 ♘xd8+ ♚h8 24 ♘f7+ ♖xf7 25 ♕b8+ ♘g8 26 ♗xf7 ♕xg4+ 27 ♚f1 ♕h3+ draws. An attempt to improve with 24 ♕d6? backfires: 24...♕xf2+!) 23 ♕d6 ♕e1+ 24 ♚d3 ♖e8 25 ♖xa8 ♘b4+ 26 ♚c4 1-0].

21...gxf6

Other moves do not help, the funniest line being 21...♖gxf6? 22 ♘g5 mate.

22 ♖he1+ ♚f7 23 ♘e5+ ♚g7 24 ♘xg6 hxg6 25 ♖xd8 ♗xd8 26 ♖d1 ♗d5 27 ♕d6 ♗b3 28 ♕xf8+ 1-0

28...♚xf8 29 ♖xd8+ ♚e7 30 ♖b8.

Kramnik – Shirov

Linares 1994

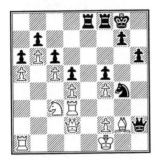

Black to play

Earlier on Black had sacrificed a piece but in the diagram position he does not have sufficient compensation. To make matters worse he must deal with the immediate threat 31 ♖h3.

30...♖f6! 31 f3

31 ♖h3? ♖g6!.

31...♖e4!

An astonishing resource, placing yet another piece *en prise*. The imagination and boldness involved captured the enthusiasm of chess commentators all over the world.

32 ♘xd5!?

Objective analysis revealed that 32 ♘e2! would have won for White. [3] But Kramnik had much to think about.

32...cxd5 33 c6 ♖xf4

33...♖xc6? 34 fxe4.

34 cxb7 ♖e4 35 ♖c1?

35 b8=♕+ ♕xb8 36 fxg4 ♖xg4 37 ♗xd5+ still favours White – Shirov.

35...♔h7 36 b8=♕ ♕xb8 37 fxg4 ♕h2 38 ♖f3 ♖xg4 39 b7? ♖fg6 40 ♖c2? ♖xg2 41 ♕xg2 ♖xg2 42 ♖xg2 ♕h1+ 43 ♔f2 ♕b1 0-1

A particular case of immense tension happens when both sides leave their pieces unprotected. The following game is a case in point.

Gufeld – Zurakov

Kiev 1959

1 e4 c5 2 ♘f3 ♘c6 3 d4 cxd4 4 ♘xd4 ♘f6 5 ♘c3 d6 6 ♗g5 e6 7 ♕d2 a6 8 0-0-0 h6 9 ♗e3 ♗e7 10 f3 ♗d7 11 g4 b5 12 a3 ♘e5 13 g5 hxg5 14 ♗xg5 ♖c8 15 f4 ♘c4 16 ♕e1 ♕b6 17 e5 dxe5 18 fxe5 ♘xb2!

Introducing hair-raising complications.

19 exf6

19 ♔xb2 b4 (19...♗xa3+?!) 20 ♘cb5 deserves consideration.

19...♘xd1

19...♗xa3 is tempting but probably incorrect. Gufeld [4] gives 20 fxg7 ♘xd1+ 21 ♔b1! (21 ♔xd1 ♕d4+) ♖g8 22 ♘d5 ♕xd4 23 ♘f6+ ♔d8 24 ♘xg8+ ♔c7 25 ♗f6!, when White defends successfully and wins.

20 ♘f5! ♗xf6! 21 ♗xf6 gxf6 22 ♘d5

White does his best to confuse the issue...

22...♕c6 23 ♗c4!

An ingenious move which guards against 23...♕xc2 mate and prepares to meet 23...bxc4 (23...♕xc4?

24 ♘d6+) with 24 ♕b4! ♕c5 25 ♘xf6+ ♔d8 26 ♖xd1!.

23...♘c3!!

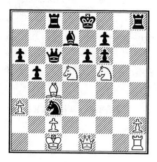

A dazzling position. Gufeld remarks that had his ♖h1 stood on g1, he could have won with 24 ♕h4! ♘e2+ 25 ♔b2, when the entire white army is 'hanging'. As it is, Black's advantage is decisive.

Unstable Pieces

Another situation, in which the level of tension increases dramatic-ally, occurs when pieces are planted on insecure posts and constant care is required.

Rashkovsky – Geller

Chigorin memorial, Sochi 1977

1 d4 ♘f6 2 c4 g6 3 ♘c3 ♗g7 4 e4 d6 5 h3 0-0 6 ♗g5 c5 7 d5 b5

Switching to a favourable variation of the Benko Gambit.

8 cxb5 a6 9 bxa6 ♕a5 10 ♗d2 ♕b4!

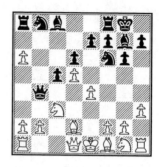

Most players would remove their queen from the a5-e1 diagonal but Geller sees that White is unable to benefit from the fact that the ♗d2 is focused on his queen.

11 ♕c2 ♗xa6 12 ♗xa6 ♘xa6 13 a3 ♕c4!

The queen enjoys very little freedom here but restricts White severely: the ♘c3 is pinned and he cannot castle.

14 ♖b1 ♘b4! 15 axb4 cxb4 16 ♘ge2 bxc3 17 ♘xc3 ♖fc8 18 f3 ♘h5 19 g4 ♘g3!

An echo of the same theme: once again a black piece ventures into the lion's den. However, White cannot exploit this fact.

20 ♖g1 ♘e2 21 ♖g2 ♘d4 22 ♕d1 ♕d3 23 ♔f2 ♘xf3 24 ♕xf3 ♕xd2+ 25 ♔g1 ♗d4+ 26 ♔h1 ♕e3 27 ♕xe3 ♗xe3

The ending is won for Black, as the white pawns are easy prey.

28 ♖c2 ♖ab8 29 ♔g2 ♖b3 30 ♖a1 ♗d4 31 ♖ac1 ♖cb8 32 ♘d1 ♔g7 33 ♖c7 ♗f6 34 ♖1c2 ♖d3 35 ♘f2 ♖e3 36 ♖a7 ♖bb3 37 ♖ac7 h6 38 ♖a7 ♗h4 39 ♖ac7 ♗xf2 40 ♖xf2 ♖xe4 41 ♖d2 ♖be3 42 ♖b7 ♖f4 0-1

Persitz – Zhidkov

Moscow 1936

1 e4 e6 2 d4 d5 3 ♘c3 ♗b4 4 e5 c5 5 a3 ♗xc3+ 6 bxc3 ♕c7 7 ♕g4 f5 8 ♗b5+?!

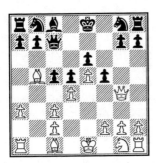

8 ♕g3 is usual. The text is rather odd and it would be intriguing to know if White, in playing it, had realized that he was committing himself to giving up material.

8...♔f8

Winning a piece as, after White's queen withdraws, 9...c4 blocks the path of retreat for the ♗b5.

Nevertheless 8...♔f7! should be preferred.

9 ♕h5 g6 10 ♕h4 c4

10...cxd4 is also tempting (11 cxd4?? ♕c3+) but one can hardly reproach Black for cutting off the bishop.

11 a4! a6 12 ♗a3+

Had Black chosen 8...♔f7, this move would have lost much of its power since it would not be accompanied by check.

12...♔f7 13 ♗d6 ♕a5

14 ♔d2!!

He is after bigger things than a repetition of moves by 14 ♗b4 ♕b6 15 ♗c5 ♕c7 16 ♗d6.

14...axb5 15 axb5! ♕xa1 16 ♕d8 ♘d7 17 ♘f3! ♕xh1 18 ♘g5+ ♔g7 19 ♘xe6+ ♔f7 20 ♘c7

Though two rooks and a bishop down, White is developing a menacing initiative. At the moment he threatens mate in three, starting with 21 e6+.

20...g5 21 ♕e8+?

A pity. White mishandles his attack and after 21...♔g7 22 ♕h5 ♘df6 23 exf6+ ♘xf6 24 ♗e5 ♕xg2 he went on to lose.

Instead, 21 e6+! would crown his grandiose concept with success: 21...♔g6 22 ♕e8+ ♔h6 23 exd7 ♘f6 24 ♗f8+ ♖xf8 25 ♕xf8+ ♔h5 (25...♔g6 26 ♕xf6+ ♔xf6 27 d8=♕+) 26 ♕f7+ ♔h4 27 ♕xf6! ♕xg2 28 ♕h6+ ♔g4 29 h3+ ♔f3 30 ♕h5+ ♔xf2 31 ♕e2+ – analysis by Konstantinopolsky. [5]

Sozin – Nekrasov

Moscow 1931

1 e4 c5 2 ♘f3 ♘f6 3 e5 ♘d5 4 b3 g6 5 ♗b2 ♗g7 6 c4 ♘c7 7 ♘c3 d6 8 exd6 exd6 9 d4 cxd4 10 ♘xd4 0-0 11 ♗e2 d5

This move, ridding himself of the weak, backward d-pawn, seems to equalize. In fact, once the d-file is cleared, Black may even train his guns against the ♘d4. However, it is not as simple as that.

12 cxd5 ♘xd5 13 ♘xd5 ♕xd5 14 0-0 ♖d8

Black creates concrete threats. White cannot bail out with 15 ♘b5 ♗xb2 16 ♘c7 because of 16...♕g5!. A prudent player would opt for 15 ♖c1, e.g. 15...♘a6 16 ♗xa6, or 15...♕a5 16 ♕c2. But there is a much stronger move:

15 ♗c4! ♕e4

Positionally Black is doing fine; but tactically he lacks a decent move. The weakness of f7 manifests itself in all variations: 15...♕c5 is met by 16 ♕f3! ♗xd4? 17 ♕xf7+ ♔h8 18 ♕f6+!.

15...♕d7 is also unsatisfactory: 16 ♕f3 ♗xd4 17 ♗xd4 ♕xd4 18 ♕xf7+ ♔h8 19 ♖ad1 ♕b6 (19...♕xd1 20 ♕f6 mate) 20 ♖xd8+ ♕xd8 21 ♖e1 ♗d7 22 ♖e8+! (neatest but 22 ♖e7 is just as effective) with mate next move.

16 ♖e1 ♕f4

16...♖xd4 17 ♗xd4 ♕xd4 18 ♖e8+. Now comes a splendid finish:

17 ♖e7! ♗xd4 18 ♖xf7! ♗xf2+ 19 ♔h1 ♖xd1+ 20 ♖xd1 1-0

A marvellous attacking miniature.

Self-pinning is something we strenuously try to avoid. In the next episode, however, White self-pins twice, with great effect.

Suba – Cebalo

Skopje 1984

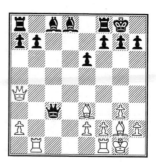

White to play

16 ♗xa7! ♗d7

An admission that he cannot take advantage of White's audacity (16...♛c7 17 ♛d4; 16...♛a5 17 ♛xa5 ♗xa5 18 ♗c5 ♖d8 19 ♗xb7 ♗xb7 20 ♖xb7 ♖d2 21 ♖fb1 h5 22 ♖7b2 – Suba).

17 ♛xd7 ♖xa7 18 ♖fc1 ♛a5 19 ♖c8 b5 20 ♗b7!

An echo of his 16th move. Once again, Black is unable to benefit from the awkward placement of White's bishop.

20...♗e7 21 ♖bc1 ♛b4 22 ♖1c7 ♖xc8 23 ♛xc8+ ♗f8 24 ♛e8! h6 25 ♛xf7+ ♔h8 26 ♛g6 ♖a4 27 ♖c8 1-0

Mutual Races

Another source of high tension occurs when a mutual race develops.

Sometimes the race is between rival pawns, dashing to promote.

Yermolinsky – Atalik

Konig Memorial,
San Francisco 2002

White to play

25 h4 ♔d7 26 h5 ♔c6 27 g4 ♘c4 28 g5

White surely seems to occupy the driver's seat.

28...♘xe3 29 fxe3 a5! 30 ♔d3

30 g6?? is premature: 30...fxg6 31 hxg6 ♖xh1 32 f7 c2. Thus White's last is an essential preparatory move.

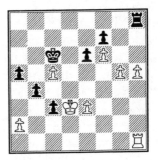

The pawn race still appears to favour White, but Black unleashes a surprise:

30...♔b5!!

By taking control of the c4 square, Black prepares some nasty threats against the white king via ...♖d8+ combined with a possible ...♔c4. Capturing on c5 allows lines in which White queens his f-pawn with check. So the black monarch cleverly uses the c5-pawn as a shield.

31 ♖h4

31 c6 ♔xc6 32 g6 is an interesting try. After 32...fxg6 33 hxg6 ♖xh1 34 f7 ♖d1+ 35 ♔c2 ♖d2+ 36 ♔c1 ♖f2 37 g7 ♖xf7 38 g8=♛ ♖f1+ 39 ♔c2 ♖f2+ 40 ♔d3 ♖d2+ 41 ♔e4 c2 it is not clear if White can win.

31...e5!

To control d4 (therefore, not 31...♖d8+ 32 ♖d4).

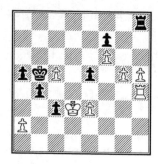

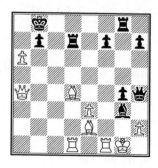

32 g6 fxg6 33 hxg6 ☖d8+

It transpires that after 34 ☗c2 ☖d2+ 35 ☗c1 ☖xa2! 36 g7 b3 White will promote first, but Black will be the first to deliver mate.

34 ☖d4! exd4 35 exd4 ☖xd4+ 36 ☗xd4 c2 37 f7 c1=☖ 38 f8=☖ ☖g1+ 39 ☗d5 ☖g5+ 40 ☗d4 ☖g1+ ½-½

Frequently a race takes place between parallel attacks on opposite wings. The fate of a battle often hangs on a single 'tempo'.

Balaish – Netzer

French junior championship 1999

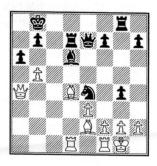

White to play

25 bxa6 ☖h4 26 g3 ☖xg3 27 fxg3 ☖xg3

28 ☗a7+!

Just as Black is about to tear White's king apart, White deals a blow which crowns his own attack first.

28...☗a8 29 axb7+ ☖xb7 30 ☗c5+ ☗b8 31 ☗d6+ ☗xd6 32 ☖xd6 ☖e7 33 ☖f4 ☖c7 34 ☖fd1 ☖c8 35 ☗xg4 ☖b2 36 ☗xc8 ☗xc8 37 ☖d8+ ☖xd8 38 ☖xd8+ ☗xd8 39 ☖d4+ 1-0

Tzesarsky – Ma. Tseitlin

Israel 2000

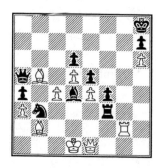

White to play

37 ☖h4

Question: ...And mates, right? Only it's Black's turn now. What should he play?

(Solution on page 141)

Chapter Three:

Coffeehouse Chess

In Reykjavik 2003, a game between Korchnoi and A.Sokolov ended in a verbal clash. At some point, says Sokolov, *"(Korchnoi) claimed that I was a coffeehouse player, playing coffeehouse chess".* [6]

'Coffeehouse chess' is an expression used by 'serious' players to describe, contemptuously, unsound play – a wild attack or a cheap trick – which does not rest upon solid positional foundations. In short, the kind of chess supposed to be played by amateurs. For example:

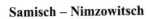

Samisch – Nimzowitsch

Baden-Baden 1925

1 d4 ♘c6 2 d5 ♘e5 3 e4 e6 4 ♘f3 ♕f6 5 ♗e2 ♗c5 6 ♘c3 a6 7 0-0 ♘g4 8 h3 h5

A premature attack, which is bound to fail. In his youth, Nimzowitsch

was sometimes inclined to experiment. This is one of his less successful brainchilds.

9 ♗g5 ♕g6 10 dxe6 fxe6 11 ♕d2 ♗e7 12 ♗f4 e5 13 ♗xe5 d6 14 ♗f4 ♗d7 15 e5 dxe5 16 hxg4 ♗d6 (16...exf4 17 ♕xd7+) **17 ♗d3 ♕f7 18 ♘xe5** and Black is totally lost (**1-0**, 50).

Also associated with 'coffeehouse chess' is cheating and lying.

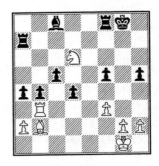

White to play

According to Brian Harley, this informal club-game proceeded: **1 ♖g3+** (!; Jumping over f3 and removing the d4-pawn *en-passant*) **♔h7 2 ♘xf8+** (!! yet another creative innovation). **2...♔h6 3 ♖g6 mate** *"finishing off with a legal mate, just to show he could do it if he liked".* [7]

Let us strip the concept 'coffeehouse chess' of its derogatory associations, wrapping it up with some positive values: spirited, fresh, uninhibited, fun-oriented chess. It is a style frequently employed by club players, who indulge in leisure activity, not in serious 'work'.

G.S. Wallis – Tsalicoglou

South African open 1964

1 e4 e5 2 ♘f3 ♘c6 3 d4 exd4 4 ♗c4 ♘f6 5 e5 d5 6 ♗b5 ♘e4 7 ♘xd4 ♗d7 8 ♗xc6 bxc6 9 ♘d2?!

A provocative move which really begs for the ensuing sacrifice.

9...♘xf2 10 ♔xf2 ♕h4+ 11 ♔e3 c5 12 ♘4f3 d4+ 13 ♔d3 ♗b5+ 14 ♘c4 ♗xc4+ 15 ♔xc4

"The ordinary player would be thoroughly unhappy (here) but George, who very seldom castles anyway, quite enjoys this sort of royal tour" – says *The South African Chessplayer*. [8]

15...♕e4 16 ♘d2 ♕c6 17 ♔d3 ♕g6+ 18 ♘e4 c4+ 19 ♔xc4 ♕xe4 20 ♖e1 ♕c6+ 21 ♔d3 ♕b5+ 22 ♔e4 ♕c6+ 23 ♔d3 ♕g6+ 24 ♔c4 ♕a6+ 25 ♔d5

It would be futile to follow this game with Fritz's commentaries. Obviously the White player is seeking a good time, rather than correct moves.

25...♖d8+ 26 ♔e4 ♕g6+ 27 ♔f3 ♗c5 28 ♕d3 ♕h5+ 29 ♔f2 0-0 30 ♔g1

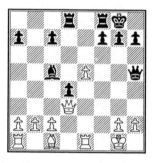

With a little help from a friend, the white king has found a safe haven. The South African magazine accompanied the last move with two exclamation marks, applauding the feat of the white monarch: *"Surely, this is the longest example of 'artificial castling' in chess history?"*

Unfortunately, after escaping the worst, White apparently lost his zeal and soon drifted into a lost position.

30...♖fe8 31 ♗f4 ♖e6 32 ♖e3 ♖b8 33 ♖h3 ♕g6 34 ♕xg6 hxg6 35 b3 d3+ 36 ♔f1 g5! 37 ♗xg5 ♖xe5 38 ♗f4 ♖f5 39 ♖f3 dxc2 40 ♖c1? ♖xf4 and **Black won**.

[On the subject of an improbable king-march, we should mention a game by the Scotsman Ian Sinclair, who had opened his last game from the world U-20 championship, Teesside 1973, with the moves 1 d3 d5 2 ♔d2 e5 3 a3 ♘f6 4 ♔c3 ♗d6

5 ♔b3 ♗e6 6 ♔a2 and still won the game. This work of art won the £1000 "Wackiest Chess Game Competition" conducted in 2005 by GM and *Daily Telegraph* chess columnist David Norwood].

Kenworthy – Ady

Sussex – Kent 1987

1 e4 c5 2 ♘f3 d6 3 c3 ♘f6 4 d3 ♘c6 5 ♘bd2 g6 6 g3 ♗g7 7 ♗g2 0-0 8 0-0 ♗d7 9 a4 a6 10 ♘c4 b5 11 axb5 axb5 12 ♖xa8 ♕xa8 13 ♘b6 ♕a2 14 ♘xd7 ♘xd7

Effortlessly, Black has acquired a very pleasant position. With his next moves, White tries to change the course of events.

15 ♗h3 ♘b6 16 d4 b4 17 d5 bxc3

This is, perhaps, overoptimistic. 17...♘a5 is safe and solid; now the game enters enormous complications.

18 dxc6 cxb2 19 ♗g5

Which will prevail: Black's advanced b-pawn or White's material advantage?

19...♘a4 20 ♗xe7 ♘c3 21 ♕xd6 b1=♕ 22 ♖xb1 ♕xb1+ 23 ♔g2 ♘xe4 24 ♗xf8 ♘xd6 25 ♗xd6

One can repeat the previous question, only with reversed colours; it is now White who has a pawn near to promotion while Black is materially up.

25...f5! 26 c7 ♕b7 27 g4 ♗f6

Stronger is 27...g5! in order to counter 28 gxf5 or 28 ♔g1 with 28...h5!.

28 gxf5 g5 29 ♔g3

Relieving the pin and preparing a nasty surprise.

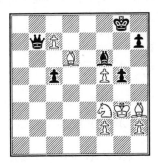

29...c4?

Oblivious of the dangers inherent in the position, Black rushes to promote a third queen. The prudent 29...h6! is required.

30 ♘xg5!

A tremendous shot. 30...♗xg5 loses to 31 f6 c3 32 ♗e6+! ♔h8 33 f7.

30...c3 31 ♗g2 ♕a6 32 ♗d5+ ♔h8

32...♔g7 33 ♘e6+ ♔h8 34 ♗f4 c2 offers more resistance. However White seems to be on top after 35 ♘c5 followed 36 ♘b3.

33 ♗f4 c2

33...♗xg5 fails to 34 c8=♕+ ♕xc8 35 ♗e5+ mating.

34 ♗e6 c1=♕ 35 ♘f7+ ♔g7 36 ♗xc1 ♕d3+ 37 ♗e3 ♗h4+ 38 ♔xh4 ♕e4+ 39 ♔g3 h5

Alert: 40...♕g4 mate is intended.

40 ♗h6+ ♔h7 41 ♘g5+ 1-0

It is a shame that White didn't have the time to promote his c-pawn, making it a five-queen game.

Nevertheless, the title "mad hacker's tea party" – under which the game first appeared in *"Kingpin"* [9] – certainly captures the game's captivating, razor-sharp, double-edged spirit. If this is what 'coffeehouse chess' is about, then let's give a big cheer.

Czerniak – Sonia Graf

Mar del Plata 1942

1 e4 ♘c6 2 d4 d5 3 e5 ♗f5 4 g4 ♗d7 5 ♘h3 e6 6 c3 ♘ce7?! 7 ♗e3 c5 8 dxc5 ♘c6 9 f4 ♘h6 10 ♗d3 ♕h4+ 11 ♘f2 0-0-0 12 ♘d2

Black's treatment of the opening leaves much to be desired. When a subsequent 13 ♘f3 is played, her game will be inferior both materially and positionally.

12...d4!?

13 ♘f3

13 cxd4 ♘xd4 14 ♗xd4 ♗c6 is an alternative intricate line.

13...dxe3

Typical 'devious chess'. The queen sacrifice is hardly sound, yet it poses White great practical difficulties. At all events, the sequel must have been more fun for Black than for White.

14 ♘xh4 exf2+ 15 ♔xf2 ♗c5+ 16 ♔g3 g5!

Black's forces, previously lacking in harmony and vitality, suddenly spring to life. Understandably, White is looking for the safest line. However, one sign of 'devious chess' is that 'safety' is seldom on the cards.

17 ♘f3

17 ♘g2 gxf4+ 18 ♔xf4 ♘xe5 19 ♔xe5 ♗c6 is one crazy possibility. 17 fxg5 ♘xe5 18 gxh6 ♗c6 19 ♗e2! seems best.

17...gxf4+ 18 ♔xf4 ♖hg8 19 g5 ♘e7! 20 c4?!

20 gxh6?? allows mate in two but 20 ♕b3 or the counter-intuitive 20 ♗xh7?! may be a better way to combat 20...♘d5+.

20...♗c6 21 ♕e2? ♖xd3! 22 ♕xd3 ♘g6+ 23 ♕xg6

A sad necessity. 23 ♔g3 ♘f5+ 24 ♔g4 ♗xf3+ regains the queen with interest.

23...fxg6 24 gxh6 ♖f8+ (0-1, 40 moves).

Day – Arencibia

Olympiad, Moscow 1994

1 e4 e6 2 ♕e2 ♘c6 3 ♕e3!? e5 4 ♗c4 ♘d4 5 ♔d1

This can hardly be designed to gain an opening advantage; rather, it wishes to upset the opponent's equanimity. Objectively White may have a decent position but one will tend not to treat his set-up seriously...

5...♘f6 6 d3 b5 7 ♗b3 a5 8 c3 ♘xb3 9 axb3 d5 10 ♔c2 ♗d6 11 ♘e2 0-0 12 ♘g3 c5 13 c4 d4 14 ♕e2 (0-1, 40 moves)

Marshall – Ed. Lasker

Second match game, USA 1923

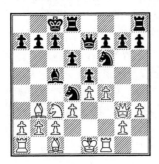

Black to play

White's last move was 11 ♖h1-f1, intending 12 fxe5 dxe5 13 ♕xg7. 11...♖hg8 was simplest, but Black opted for something else:

11...♘f5!?

The start of a long-range plan, involving a piece sacrifice. The knight cannot be captured right away (12 exf5? exf4+) but it will eventually fall.

"I was perfectly aware of the fact that the sacrifice might not stand up under analysis" – writes Edward Lasker – *"but I also realized that Marshall would have to defend himself most carefully for a long while, something I knew to be most distasteful to him".* [10]

12 ♕g5 g6 13 fxe5 ♕xe5 14 ♕f4 ♕e7 15 g4 d5 16 gxf5 g5! 17 ♕f3 dxe4 18 dxe4 ♗b4 19 ♗xg5

19 ♗d2 ♖xd2! 20 ♔xd2 ♘xe4+ with a powerful attack.

19...♖hg8 20 ♗h4 ♖d4 21 ♗d5?

21 ♗e6+! fxe6 22 fxe6 ♕xe6 23 ♗xf6 refutes Black's scheme.

21...♖e8 22 ♗xf6 ♕xf6 23 ♖d1 c6 24 ♖xd4 ♕xd4 25 a3? ♗xc3+ 26 bxc3 ♕xd5 (0-1, 50 moves)

The essence of 'coffeehouse chess' is that

1) it is often unsound;

2) its practitioners are well aware of its unsoundness; and

3) they don't care.

Saying that, it is hardly surprising that coffeehouse chess is frequently employed in blitz-games. This form of speed chess is backed up by a tailor-made philosophy. Here is what one prominent exponent of blitz preaches: *"I transfer the risk of making the decisions to my opponent... I keep myself away from resolving particular positions, give my opponent the widest possible choice of opportunities and hope he marries the wrong woman"* – the late Genrikh Chepukaitis. [11]

...And we haven't yet mentioned the special 'techniques' of choosing to move with the piece closest to the clock, or – in internet chess – 'pre-moving' (executing an extra move *before* our opponent has made his move).

No wonder that fast chess abounds in random displays of gambling and rambling.

Chepukaitis – Bagirov

Baku 1957 (Blitz game)

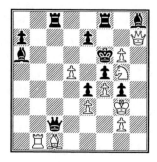

White to play

White has shed a great deal of material to obtain a crushing attack. In the diagram position he can cash in his investments with 1 ♕h6, when the deadly threats of 2 ♘h7 mate and 2 g7+ are decisive, leading quickly to mate.

**1 ♗b2+? ♖c3 2 ♖a1 ♗f1!
3 ♗xc3+ ♕xc3 4 ♖xf1?**

White can still revert to the correct path with 4 ♕h6.

4...♕xe3+ 5 ♔h4 ♗g7 6 ♔h5!

A fascinating and picturesque scene. The white monarch is not only running for his life but also chasing his counterpart. His last move creates the threat of 7 ♕g8!! ♖xg8 8 ♘h7 mate.

6...♕g3?

6...♖h8 is much stronger, virtually winning for Black; although the lady is taboo, the pin forestalls further offensive actions.

7 ♖c1 ♕xf4

Or 7...♕h2+ 8 ♘h3 ♖d8 (else 9 ♖c6+) 9 ♕g8!. After the text move, 8 ♕xg7+ ♔xg7 9 ♘e6+ fails to 9...♔f6 10 ♘xf4 ♖h8 mate.

8 ♖c6+ ♕d6

An astute, albeit forced defence, banking on 9 ♖xd6+ exd6 10 ♘f7 (otherwise 10...♖h8) 10...e3 and the pawn queens.

**9 ♘f7 ♕xc6 10 dxc6 e3 11 ♘h6!
♖h8**

The alternative is 11...e2 12 ♘g8+ ♖xg8 13 ♕xg8 e1=♕ 14 ♕f7+ ♔e5 15 ♕xe7+ followed by 16 ♕xe1.

In the line which occurs in the game, fresh queens are reborn and White is ahead in the mutual race.

**12 ♕xh8 ♗xh8 13 c7 e2 14 c8=♕
e1=♕ 15 ♕xf5+ ♔g7 16 ♕f7 mate**

13...Rd7!

Intending to double rooks on the d-file. In doing so, he blocks, *en passant*, the c8-h3 diagonal. Surprisingly, this fact has far reaching implications...

14 Qxg4?

...which White fails to spot. Due to Black's 13th move, the queen capture is no longer accompanied by a check. This makes the following combination possible:

14...Bxh2+! 15 Kxh2 Nxg4+ 16 Kg3 Nxe3 17 Rxe3 Rxd2

Black has emerged from this forced series of moves with a winning advantage.

18 b4 h5 19 Rf3 f6 20 a4 Re8 21 Kh4 Rd5 22 Rg3 Re4+ 23 Kh3 g5 0-1

You Cannot Be Serious

Some moves are so outrageous and rule-breaking that one finds it hard to treat them with respect.

D. Bronstein – Prameshuber

Krems 1967

Black to play

20...Bxa2!?

True, the bishop is temporarily safe, as 21 Nxa2 is met by 21...Bxd2; but after White's next move, the intruder's future seems bleak: *"When my opponent made his surprising 20th move, I took it as a joke"* – D. Bronstein. [12]

21 b3 Rcd8

He intends to exact a significant price for his bishop: 22 Ra1 Bxb3 23 cxb3 Qxd3.

22 Re3 a5 23 Qf2?!

Bronstein reveals that during the game he envisaged 23...Bxc3 24 Bxc3 a4 25 h4 axb3 26 h5 g5 27 h6. He later regretted skipping the line 23 Qe2 Bxc3 24 Bxc3 a4 25 Rg3 axb3 26 Rxg6.

23...Bxb3 24 cxb3 Bc5 25 Rfe1 Qxd3

In this way Black obtains a decent return for his investment.

26 Rxd3 Bxf2 27 Rxd8 Rxd8 28 Re2 Bd4 29 g3 Be5 30 Na4 b6 31 Bc3 Rd3 32 Rc2 b5 33 Bxa5 bxa4 34 bxa4 Rd4 35 Rxc6 Rxa4 36 Bxc7 Bxc7 37 Rxc7 Rxe4 38 h4 Re2 39 Kg1 Nf8 40 Kf1 Re7 41 Rc8+ ½-½

Granda Zuniga – Seirawan

Buenos Aires 1993

1 Nf3 Nf6 2 c4 c5 3 Nc3 e6 4 g3 b6 5 Bg2 Bb7 6 0-0 Nc6 7 e4 e5 8 d3 g6

Chapter Four:

Not So Elementary, My Dear Watson

One element that characterizes unconventional chess is its freshness. Moves are often surprising and certainly not obvious; whether the players belong to the logical school or arrive at their conclusions through intuition, 'devious' moves do not easily suggest themselves.

Not Your First Choice

Bogolyubov – Rellstab

1940

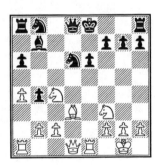

White to play

Bearing in mind the frailty of the Nd6, our first thought is probably 15 Nxd6+ Qxd6 16 Bb5+, attacking both king and queen.

Alas, with the forced 16...Ke7, Black avoids the worst; queen exchanges are imminent and a large part of White's advantage vanishes.

A refinement of the basic idea is required:

15 Bg6!!

Now 15...Nxc4 fails to 16 Rxe6+; likewise, after 15...Be7 16 Nxd6 Qxd6 17 Qxd6+ Kxd6 18 Bxf7 Bd5 19 Rad1, Black is torn apart.

15...hxg6 16 Nxd6+ Ke7 17 Nxb7 Qc7 18 Qd5 Rh5 19 Qe4 Nc6 20 g4 1-0

Camara – Mangini

Brazilian championship 1958

1 d4 d5 2 Nf3 Nf6 3 c4 c6 4 Nc3 e6 5 Bg5 dxc4 6 e4 Qa5

The modern continuation is 6...b5 7 e5 h6.

7 Bxf6 gxf6 8 Bxc4 Bg7 9 Qe2 0-0 10 0-0 Qh5

Let us ponder over the diagram position for a while.

White has an edge: his pawn structure is superior, his forces cooperate harmoniously, his pieces are better developed. Reasonable candidate moves might be 11 ♗d3 (to discourage ...f5); 11 a4 (to hinder any black queenside expansion) or 11 d5 (opening the game to exploit his lead in development) among others. I wonder how many readers would contemplate the move White actually chose in the game...

11 g4!?

Whether or not the move is analytically the best, one cannot but appreciate its audacity.

11...♕xg4+ 12 ♔h1 ♘d7 13 ♖g1 ♕h5?

The critical line is 13...♕f4. White would generate strong pressure along the g-file but Black may possess adequate defensive resources. The text move loses by force.

14 ♖g3 ♔h8 15 ♖ag1 ♖g8

15...♗h6 is countered by the same deadly rejoinder.

16 ♘e5! 1-0

Routine Moves, Vicious Intentions

Some moves have a perfectly innocent appearance. They can easily be misinterpreted as innocuous, while in fact they are poisonous.

R. Moor – Jenni

Switzerland 2001

1 e4 e5 2 ♘f3 ♘c6 3 ♗b5 a6 4 ♗a4 ♘f6 5 ♕e2 ♗e7 6 c3 b5 7 ♗b3 0-0 8 0-0 d5 9 d3 ♗b7 10 ♖e1 ♖e8 11 ♘bd2 ♘f8 12 a3 h6 13 h3 ♕d7 14 ♘h2 ♖ad8 15 ♘g4 ♘xg4 16 hxg4 d4

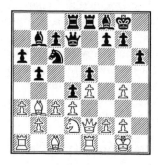

Let us take the diagram as a starting point for our analysis. Black's d5-pawn was attacked and he chose to advance it. Now his pawn is no longer in danger. Is Black threatening anything? Yes, to win a pawn by 17...dxc3 18 bxc3 ♕xd3.

White has several viable options: 17 c4, ♗d5, 17 ♗c2, 17 ♕f3.

Question: What should White play? **Hint:** ask yourself whether 17...dxc3 is Black's only threat.

Vera – Herrera

Ubeda 2001

1 ♘f3 c5 2 c4 ♘c6 3 d4 cxd4 4 ♘xd4 ♘f6 5 ♘c3 e6 6 g3 ♕b6 7 ♘db5 d5 8 ♗g2 d4 9 ♘a4 ♕a5+ 10 ♗d2 ♕d8 11 e3 e5 12 exd4 exd4

13 0-0

Apparently an innocuous move, aiming solely at completing his development; but it contains an additional, concealed aim which Black fails to spot.

13...a6? 14 ♕e1+!

White's previous move vacated this square for his queen. Now she supports the dark-squared bishop to form a lethal battery.

14...♗e6 15 ♗xc6+ bxc6 16 ♗a5

Black suffers heavy material losses and lost on the 24ᵗʰ move.

Veresov – D. Bronstein

Moscow 1960

Black to play

Black has sacrificed a pawn to obtain this position. The unnatural

placing of the white monarch certainly offers some compensation.

16...♗e4!

In itself this move is hardly lethal, but one of its fine points is that it is quite difficult to fathom its intention.

17 ♖hd1?

17 ♕b3 c5 18 a3 a4 is unconvincing, but 17 ♖f1, intending 18 ♘e1, is better.

17...h6!

We assume that the majority of readers are still vague about Black's plan.

18 ♗h3 ♗h7!

Only now does it become evident: Black prepares a deadly battery along the b1-h7 diagonal with 19...♕g6. By now, it may well be too late for White to save the game.

19 ♖d7 ♖fe8 20 ♔d2 ♗f5! 21 ♕

Capitulation, but 21 ♗xf5 also loses shortly.

21...♗xh3 22 ♕xf6 gxf6 0

Del Rio – Minasi

Ubeda 2001

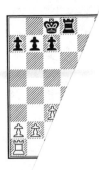

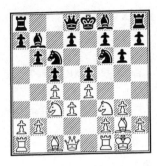

9 ♘xe5!?

An inspired piece sacrifice, based on purely positional grounds. The white pawns start rolling, the black pieces must withdraw from their posts.

Can this be right? Any Black player would see it as his duty to refute such a sacrifice (as he would treat other dubious lines, such as 1 e4 e5 2 ♘f3 ♘f6 3 ♘xe5 d6 4 ♘xf7?!; or 1 e4 e5 2 ♘f3 ♘c6 3 ♘c3 ♘f6 4 ♘xe5?! ♘xe5 5 d4 ♘g6 6 e5 ♘g8).

But in a practical game, it is far from an easy task.

9...♘xe5 10 f4 ♘c6

Sometimes, following a sacrificial offer, the defending side chooses to return material. In the present context, returning material would not relieve Black's game: 10...♗d6 (10...d6?? 11 fxe5 dxe5 12 ♗g5 ♗e7 13 ♕f3) 11 fxe5 ♗xe5 12 ♗h6.

11 e5 ♘g8 12 f5 ♘h6

12...♖b8 13 e6 dxe6 14 fxe6 f5 is a probable improvement.

13 ♘e4 ♘xf5 14 ♘f6+ ♔e7 15 ♘d5+ ♔e8 16 ♘f6+ ♔e7

Following his bold sacrifice, White already has a draw in hand; but he aspires for more!

17 g4 ♘fd4 18 ♕e1 ♕b8 19 ♘d5+ ♔d8 20 ♗g5+ ♔c8 21 ♖xf7 ♘e6 22 ♗f6 ♘cd8?

22...♖g8!, with ideas like ...♘cd4 and ...♗c6, is better.

23 ♖e7 ♖g8 24 ♖e8

An amazing infiltration which proves decisive.

24...♗c6 25 ♗xd8 ♘xd8 26 ♘f6 ♖h8 27 ♗xc6 dxc6 28 ♕e4 ♕c7 29 e6 ♗g7 30 e7 ♖xe8 31 ♘xe8 ♗d4+ 32 ♔h1 ♕d7 33 ♘d6+ ♕xd6 34 e8=♕ a5 35 ♖f1 ♖a7 36 ♖f8 ♖d7 37 ♕4e6 ♕xe6 38 ♕xe6 ♔c7 39 ♕e2 ♗g7 40 ♖f2 ♗d4 41 ♖f3 ♘f7

Black's position is hard to crack but in the long run White's material advantage is bound to tell.

42 ♖f4 ♘d6 43 ♔g2 ♘c8 44 b3 ♖e7 45 ♖e4 ♖f7 46 ♕e1 ♖d7 47 ♕g3+ ♔b7 48 h3 ♖f7 49 h4 ♖d7 50 ♖e6 ♗c3 51 ♕f3 ♘d6 52 ♕f8 ♘c8 53 ♖e8 ♖c7 54 ♖d8 ♗g7 55 ♕e8 ♗f6 56 ♖xc8 1-0

Is This Move Really Possible?

The following examples illustrate situations where a move is so surprising and extraordinary that one suspects there may be something wrong with the initial position.

Hottes – H.Hoffmann

Heilbronn 1964

White to play

1 ♘g5 ♗xe2 2 ♘xf7?!

2 ♕xe2 0-0 3 ♗e3 or 3 ♖d1 is a promising continuation; but White believes that he can achieve more. In addition to forking queen and rook, the text move threatens mate in one.

2...♕b6? 3 ♕xe2 0-0 4 d6! ♖xf7 5 ♕c4 and White won.

Castling is a very common move in chess; there is in fact a chess book by Timmer, devoted exclusively to this subject. [13] However, in the diagram position, castling appears to be a peculiar idea. Nevertheless, 2...0-0!! turns the tables in Black's favour, as it wins a piece and the game: 3 ♘xd8 ♗xd1, or 3 ♕xe2 ♖xf7.

Taimanov – Zakhodiakin

USSR 1945

1 e4 e5 2 ♘f3 ♘c6 3 ♗b5 a6 4 ♗a4 d6 5 c3 f5 6 exf5 ♗xf5 7 d4 e4 8 ♘g5 d5 9 f3 e3 10 f4

A series of strange moves which have actually been tested in many practical games.

10...♗d6 11 ♗xe3 ♕e7 12 ♕e2 ♗d3?!

12...♘f6 or 12...♘h6 is preferable. Black's move contains a shrewd idea but is refuted tactically.

13 ♕xd3 ♗xf4

14 ♘f7!!

Where does this come from? Unlike 2 ♘xf7?! in the previous game, here the knight leap is devastating: White wins in all variations: 14...♕xf7 15 ♖f1! (not 15 0-0? ♗xe3+) g5 16 g3; or 14...♔xf7 15 ♕f5+ ♘f6 16 ♕xf4 ♖ae8 17 ♔d2; or 14...♗xe3 15 ♘xh8 ♗c1+ 16 ♔d1 ♗xb2 17 ♖e1.

I. Rogers – Smerdon

Caloundra Australian club championship 2003

1 e4 e6 2 d4 d5 3 ♘c3 ♘f6 4 ♗g5 ♗b4 5 e5 h6 6 ♗d2 ♗xc3 7 bxc3 ♘e4 8 ♕g4 g6 9 ♗d3 ♘xd2 10 ♔xd2 c5 11 h4 ♘c6 12 ♘f3 cxd4 13 cxd4 ♕a5+ 14 c3 b6 15 ♕f4 ♗a6 16 ♕f6? ♖g8 17 ♗xa6 ♕xa6 18 ♖hc1 ♘a5

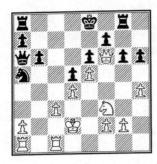

White has handled this complex MacCutcheon variation of the French Defence in an inaccurate manner. As a consequence, Black has a very comfortable position.

19 ♔e1 ♘c4 20 ♖ab1

Such a move is seldom played voluntarily. Black threatened 20...♘b2!, while 20 ♖c2 ♘a3 is inconvenient.

20...♕xa2 21 ♔f1 ♘a3?!

A turning point. 21...♘d2+ 22 ♘xd2 ♕xd2 is correct; instead, Black aspires to increase his gains.

22 ♖a1 ♕b3 23 ♔g1 ♖c8?

Natural, but faulty.

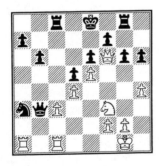

24 c4!!

Astonishingly, White breaks through Black's most fortified outpost: c4. Black is short of a

satisfactory capture: 24...♘xc4? 25 ♖xa7; 24...dxc4? 25 d5! exd5 26 e6; 24...♖xc4 25 ♘d2.

24...♕b2 25 ♖cb1! ♕c3 26 cxd5 ♘xb1 27 ♖xa7 ♖c7 28 ♖a8+ ♖c8 29 dxe6

Much stronger than 29 d6 ♔d7.

29...♕c1+ 30 ♔h2 ♖f8 31 exf7+ ♖xf7 32 ♕e6+ ♔d8 33 ♖xc8+ ♕xc8 34 ♕xf7 (1-0, 42 moves)

Lastly, there are occasions where we wonder incredulously whether a move is *legal*:

From a study by G. Kasparyan

Published posthumously

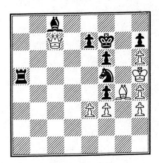

White to play and draw

1 ♕c4+

The threat of 1...♘g3 mate doesn't leave White much choice, as 1 ♗xf5 ♖xf5+ 2 ♔g4 ♖c5+ loses on the spot.

1...♗e6 2 ♕xe6+ ♔xe6 3 e4 ♔d6

Or 3...♔d7 (f7). 3...♔e5 4 ♗xf5 ♔d4 5 ♔g4 is an alternative draw. In the latter case, Black is reduced to 5...♖xf5 6 exf5 ♔e3 7 ♔h5 ♔xf3 stalemate.

4 exf5

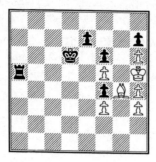

Now what? To lift the stalemate, Black must play 4...e5, right? Well, it is still a stalemate, as the *en passant* capture 5 fxe6 is illegal!

"One has to look at the position several times before being convinced of the reality of the stalemate. Probably no textbook definitions of pin and unpin take account of the present case" – John Roycroft. [14]

Chapter Five:

Peculiar Moves

Conventional chess abounds in tactics of a basic nature: pin, fork, double-attack, deflection. 'Devious chess' is more subtle: hereunder are some of its seldom seen devices.

One Move Gains Two Pieces

Motwani – Hendriks

Vlissingen 1996

1 c4 g6 2 d4 ♝g7 3 ♞c3 d6 4 e4 ♞d7 5 ♞f3 e5 6 ♝e3 ♞gf6 7 ♝e2 0-0 8 d5 ♞g4 9 ♝d2 f5 10 ♞g5 ♞df6 11 exf5 gxf5 12 h3 ♞h6 13 g4! ♚h8?

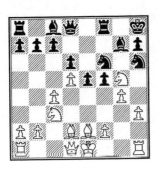

14 ♞e6! ♝xe6 15 g5!

White is temporarily a piece down but cannot be prevented from winning two pieces in a row. The unfortunate placement of the black king robs the ♝g7 of a flight square.

15...♞hg8 16 gxf6 ♛xf6 17 dxe6 ♛xe6 18 ♛b3 b6 19 c5 ♛xb3 20 axb3 bxc5 21 ♞b5 ♜fc8 22 ♝a5 1-0

Grigoriev – Panikovsky

Kurgan 1972

1 e4 c5 2 ♞c3 ♞c6 3 g3 g6 4 ♝g2 ♝g7 5 d3 d6 6 f4 ♞h6 7 ♞f3 f5 8 0-0 0-0 9 h3 ♞f7 10 ♝e3 ♞d4 11 ♛d2 ♜b8 12 ♝f2? fxe4

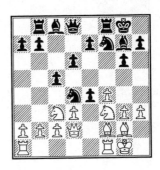

13 ♞xd4

White tries to avoid the loss of a pawn after 13 dxe4 (♞xe4) ♞xf3+ 14 ♝xf3 ♝xh3, but suffers a deeper fall:

13...e3!

As in the former example, we witness an extraordinary *zwischenzug*, which gains two pieces in succession.

14 ♘e6 exf2+ 0-1

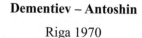

Dementiev – Antoshin

Riga 1970

1 e4 e5 2 ♘f3 d6 3 d4 exd4 4 ♘xd4 ♘f6 5 ♘c3 ♗e7 6 ♗e2 0-0 7 0-0 a6 8 ♗f4 c5 9 ♘f3 ♗e6 10 ♘g5 ♘c6 11 ♘xe6 fxe6 12 ♗c4 ♕c8 13 ♘a4 ♘xe4 14 ♕g4 d5 15 ♘b6 ♘f6 16 ♕h3 ♕d8 17 ♘xa8

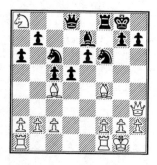

Black can now regain a piece with 17...♕xa8 or 17...dxc4, but he would still be left materially worse.

17...e5!!

An incredible idea: Instead of capturing a piece, Black chooses to remain a rook down and menaces a third white piece. Inevitably, he now increases his gains.

18 ♕e6+ ♔h8 19 ♗xe5 dxc4 20 ♗xf6 ♗xf6 21 ♕xc4 ♕xa8 22 c3 b6 23 ♖ad1 ♘e5 (0-1, 37 moves)

Long, Long Moves

Pietzsch – Larsen

Dortmund 1961

White to play

White has sacrificed a piece to reach this threatening position. However, Black's defences seem to be sturdy: 22 ♕h2? ♕xg6 (or 22...♕xe3+ 24 ♖d2 ♕e1+=); or 22 ♖h8+? ♔xh8 23 ♕h2+ ♕h6.

22 ♖xd5!? ♖xf1+!

22...♕xd5?? allows 23 ♖h8+ ♔xh8 24 ♕h2+. The text move, one of many 'long' moves we are about to witness, deflects the white rook from the h-file, while increasing, *en passant*, his material gains.

23 ♖xf1 ♕xd5 24 ♕h2 ♗f5 25 ♕h7+ ♔f8 26 g4

White has indeed built up a strong attack, but Black's resources are more than adequate.

26...♘d3+ 27 ♔b1 ♘f2+ 28 ♔a1 ♖d8?

Black begins to slip. 28...♘xg4! 29 ♕h8+ ♔e7! grants him a winning advantage: 30 ♕xa8 ♘e3 31 ♖e1 ♗e4; or 30 ♕xg7+ ♔d6.

29 ♕h8+ ♕g8 30 ♕h4! ♔e8?

Another half a point goes down the drain. 30...♕d5! 31 ♕h8+ ♕g8 (31...♔e7!?) is equal.

31 gxf5 ♖d2

32 ♕a4+!

Some moves are hard to foresee. Long moves are one such example...

32...♔d8?

32...♔e7! and if 33 ♖xf2? then 32...♕c4!!.

33 ♖xf2! ♖xf2 34 ♕h4+! 1-0

...And switch-backs are yet another one. When a long move is combined with a switch-back, it is often deadly.

S. Brown – J. Howell

Calderdale 1993

1 d4 ♘f6 2 ♘f3 g6 3 ♘bd2 c5 4 e3 ♗g7 5 ♗d3 d5 6 b3 ♘c6 7 ♗b2 cxd4 8 ♘xd4 ♕c7 9 ♘xc6 bxc6 10 c4 0-0 11 cxd5 cxd5 12 ♖c1 ♕d6 13 ♘f3 ♘e4?!

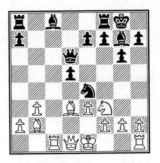

14 ♗xg7 ♕b4+?

Probably expecting 15 ♘d2 ♔xg7 16 ♗xe4 dxe4 17 ♖c4 ♕a5 with complications. It was difficult to realize that, though remote, the far-away ♗g7 is still alive; it now returns with venom:

15 ♗c3! ♘xc3 16 a3!

Certainly not 16 ♕d2? ♘xa2!; but now, if the black queen withdraws to a5, 17 ♕d2 decides.

16...♘xd1+ 17 axb4 ♘b2 18 ♗e2 a5

Desperation. 18...♗f5 19 ♔d2 with ♘d4 to follow is equally hopeless.

19 ♖b1 axb4 20 ♖xb2 ♖a1+ 21 ♗d1 ♗a6 22 ♔d2 ♖c8 23 ♖e1 1-0

And then, in the Midst of the Storm... the King Moves

Dzindzichashvili – Tseshkovsky

USSR championship, first league, Tbilisi 1973

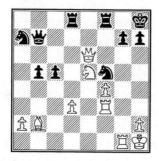

White to play

31 ♖xg7!!

A stunning sacrifice which sets the board on fire. The intrusive rook may be captured in three different ways.

31...♘xg7

31...♕xg7? allows mate by 32 ♘g6+ hxg6 33 ♖h3+ ♘h6 34 ♖xh6. 31...♔xg7 is probably best, when White can force a draw with 32 ♘d7+ ♘d4 33 ♕e7+ ♔h8 (33...♖f7? 34 ♕g5+) 34 ♕e5+. However, the text move should not lose.

32 ♔g1!!

Quietly sidestepping the pin. Obviously the white queen is taboo: 32...♘xe6? 33 ♘f7++ ♔g8 34 ♘h6 mate.

32...♖d4

32...♖f5 is a sound alternative: 33 ♕h6 (33 ♖g3 ♖d4 34 ♕h6 ♖h5 35 ♕f6 ♖f5 36 ♕h6=) ♔g8 34 ♖h3 ♖h5 35 ♖xh5 ♘xh5 36 ♕xh5 (36 ♕e6+ ♔f8=) ♕g7 with an unclear position.

33 ♗xd4 cxd4 34 ♕h6 ♔g8

34...♖c8; 34...♖e8, and 34...♖f5 all lead to a draw.

35 ♖h3 ♘f5 36 ♕e6+ ♔g7 37 ♘d7 ♕c8 38 ♘xf8 ♕c1+?

An error. It was still a draw after 38...♔xf8.

39 ♔g2 ♕d2+

Or 39...♘e3+ 40 ♖xe3 dxe3 41 ♕e7+ ♔g8 42 ♘e6 ♕c6+ 43 ♔g3 curtains.

40 ♔g1 ♕d1+ 41 ♔f2 1-0

The checks run out after 41...♕d2+ 42 ♔f3 ♕xd3+ 43 ♔g4 ♘e3+ 44 ♔g5 ♔xf8 45 ♖h6.

Zalts – Bludshtein

Israeli championship, semi finals 1996

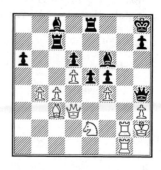

White to play

32 c5 exf4 33 ♕d4! ♖f7 34 ♘xf4 ♗xd4

White threatened 35 ♘g6+, so Black is forced, willy-nilly, to accept the gift.

35 ♗xd4+ ♖f6

It is not immediately clear how White should proceed.

36 ♔h1!!

A quiet king move following a queen sacrifice. Black is defenceless against 37 ♖g5. White's last move was a necessary preparatory move, as the immediate 36 ♖g5 fails to 36...♕xf4 *check*.

Black is so entangled that he cannot make his material advantage tell, even though it is his turn.

36...♖f8 37 ♖g5 ♕xg5

The alternatives are cheerless: 37...h6 38 ♗xf6+; 37...h5 38 ♘g6+; 37...♕h6 38 ♘h5.

38 ♖xg5 h6 39 ♖g6 1-0

The Pawn Wedge

Shifting pieces from one wing to the other is a familiar device, occurring in almost every game. Whenever we wish to strengthen our attack, create a shield for our king, or just change our plans, we alter the placement of our pieces.

Driving a wedge inside our opponent's territory is frequently a powerful idea. In such a case, play continues, in effect, on only one wing; we can mobilize all our forces while our poor opponent cannot cross the wedge to rush over reinforcements.

Huzman – Minasian

European championship, Pula 1997

1 d4 ♘f6 2 ♘f3 c5 3 d5 g6 4 ♘c3 ♗g7 5 e4 0-0 6 e5 ♘g4 7 ♗g5 ♘h6

7...♘xe5? 8 f4.

8 h4 f6 9 ♘ge4 ♘f7 10 h5 f5 11 ♘g5 ♘xg5 12 ♗xg5 ♗xe5 13 hxg6 hxg6 14 d6!

Refuting Black's dubious set-up. The d6-pawn is a killer: 14...♗xd6? 15 ♗c4+ wins instantly.

14...♗f6 15 ♗xf6 ♖xf6 16 ♗c4+ e6 17 ♕d2 ♕f8?

17...♖f7 is more stubborn.

18 ♘d5! exd5 19 ♗xd5+ ♖e6+ 20 ♗xe6+ dxe6 21 ♕g5 ♗d7 22 0-0-0 ♗e8 23 ♕d8 1-0

Hecht – Keller

Zurich 1966

White to play

Gusev – Aurbach

USSR 1946

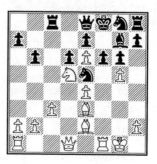

White to play

The d3-pawn is a thorn in White's flesh. Naturally he tries to remove it...

11 f4?

...but fails beautifully:

11...♕b6+ 12 ♔h1 h5! 13 ♖e3

It transpires that 13 fxe5 is answered by 13...♗g4! 14 ♕b3 (14 hxg4? hxg4 mate) ♕f2, when 15 ♖d1, loses to 15...♖h6! 16 ♗xd3 ♗f3! 17 ♖g1 ♕g3!.

13...♘c4 14 ♖g3 ♗g4! 15 ♕e1 ♘xb2! 16 ♕e3 ♘d1! 17 ♕xb6 axb6 18 hxg4

18 ♗xd3 h4!; 18 ♖xg4 ♘f2+ 19 ♔g1 is the lesser evil.

18...hxg4+ 19 ♔g1 d5! 20 ♗xd3

Finally White gets rid of this dreadful pawn. Alas, by now the damage is already beyond repair.

20...♗c5+ 21 ♔f1 dxe4 22 ♗c2

Or 22 ♗xe4 ♘f2.

22...♗f2 0-1

23 ♖xg4 ♖h1+ 24 ♔e2 ♖e1 mate.

Black is in dire straits. Strangled by the e6-pawn, White finds a remarkable way of finishing him off.

19 ♘xf6 ♘xf6

19...exf6 20 ♕xd6+ followed by 21 ♕xe5 is easy.

20 gxf6 ♗xf6 21 ♗h6+ ♔g8 22 ♖xf6! exf6 23 ♕xd6 ♖c6 24 ♕xe5!! fxe5 25 ♖f1

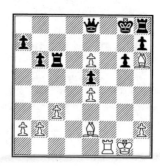

25...♖c8

Despite his huge material advantage, Black is helpless. The text move is directed against 26 ♗b5. 25...♖xe6 loses to 26 ♗c4 with the unstoppable 27 ♗xe6+ and 28 ♖f8 mate to follow.

26 ♗d1! ♖c4 27 ♗b3 b5 28 ♗xc4 bxc4 29 b3

29 b4 is clearer; anyway, with Black's king's flank paralyzed, the advance of White's infantry on the other flank will eventually decide.

29...a5 30 bxc4 ♕e7 31 ♔g2 ♕a3 32 ♖f2 ♕e7 33 ♖f1 g5 34 c5 ♕d8

34...♕xc5 35 ♖f7 ♕a3 36 ♖f5.

35 c6 ♕e7 36 c7 1-0

Birnboim – Dzindzichashvili

Netanya 1977

1 d4 ♘f6 2 c4 g6 3 ♘c3 ♗g7 4 e4 d6 5 ♘f3 0-0 6 ♗e2 ♗g4 7 ♗e3 ♘fd7 8 ♘g1 ♗xe2 9 ♘gxe2 c5 10 0-0 ♘c6 11 d5 ♘a5 12 b3 a6 13 ♖b1 ♘f6 14 ♕d3 ♘g4 15 ♗g5 ♘e5 16 ♕h3 ♖e8 17 f4 ♘d7 18 ♕h4

Black's exceedingly passive play allows White to build up an attack, which soon proves decisive.

18...b5 19 e5 f6 20 ♗h6 f5 21 ♖f3 b4 22 ♖h3 ♘f8

23 ♗xg7 ♔xg7 24 ♕h6+ ♔g8 25 ♘e4! fxe4 26 e6

This pawn is worth more than a whole piece. Black's queenside is irrelevant and White wins at his leisure.

26...♘c6 27 f5 ♘e5 28 fxg6 ♘g4 29 gxh7+ ♔h8 30 ♕g7+! 1-0

Sutovsky – S. Movsesian

Ohrid 2001

White to play

White discovers a brilliant winning method:

48 ♖e7!! ♘xd5 49 ♖e8! ♘f4 50 ♖xf8+ ♕xf8 51 ♕e8 ♘g6 52 b4! ♔h7 53 ♕xf8 ♘xf8 54 bxc5

The f7-pawn contains Black's king while his knight cannot cope with both passed pawns on its own.

54...♘e6 55 c6 1-0

Blocking Escape Routes

Winning material is usually accomplished by straightforward means. In 'unconventional chess' it is sometimes executed differently:

instead of directly hitting an enemy officer, one first deprives it of flight squares and only then traps it.

Dely – Varnuz

Hungarian championship 1961

1 e4 c5 2 ♘f3 e6 3 d4 cxd4 4 ♘xd4 ♘c6 5 ♘c3 ♕c7 6 f4 a6 7 a3 d6 8 ♗e3 ♘f6 9 ♕f3 ♘a5 10 ♘b3 ♘c4? 11 ♗xc4 ♕xc4

12 ♗c5!!

An original and attractive move, based on the tactical 12...dxc5 13 ♘a5 ♕d4 14 ♖d1. If Black does not react swiftly, 13 0-0-0, coupled with 14 ♖d4, decides.

12...a5 13 e5 a4 14 ♗xd6 axb3

14...♗xd6 15 ♘d2 ♕a6 may be the lesser evil.

15 ♗xf8 ♔xf8 16 cxb3 ♕xb3 17 exf6 gxf6 18 ♖d1 ♕b6 19 ♘e4 ♕a5+ 20 b4 ♕f5 21 0-0 ♔g7 22 ♘g3 ♕g6 23 ♘h5+ ♔h6 24 g4 (1-0, 30 moves)

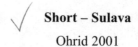

Short – Sulava

Ohrid 2001

1 e4 d5 2 exd5 ♕xd5 3 ♘c3 ♕d6 4 d4 ♘f6 5 ♗e3 ♗f5? 6 ♕f3 ♗c8 7 0-0-0 c6 8 ♗f4 ♕b4 9 ♘ge2 ♗e6?

Completely oblivious to the impending danger.

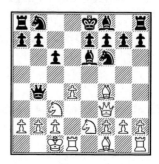

Question: How can White benefit from the position of the black queen?

Nikolov – Delchev

Bled 1997

Black to play

18...♗xf3! 19 ♗xf8 ♗xf8 20 ♗xf3 ♘e5

By forking rook and knight, it seems that Black gains material.

21 ♖d5 ♘xf3+ 22 ♔g2

Now it looks as if it is White who holds the upper hand, as the black knight is lost.

However, Black now performs a rare tactic: he utilizes the doomed knight to deflect the white rook to the kingside, where it will be imprisoned by the black infantry.

22...♘g5! 23 ♖xg5 f5!

White faces inevitable material loses.

24 b3 ♖b6 25 ♖d1 h6 26 ♖xg6+ ♖xg6 27 ♖d5 ♗b4 28 ♖xf5 ♖c6 29 a3 ♖c5 30 ♖xc5 ♗xc5 31 b4 ♗xb4 (0-1, 38 moves)**

Dreev – Tiviakov

USSR championship, Moscow 1991

1 d4 ♘f6 2 c4 e6 3 ♘f3 b6 4 ♘c3 ♗b7 5 a3 d5 6 cxd5 ♘xd5 7 ♕c2 ♘xc3 8 ♕xc3 ♘d7 9 ♗g5 ♗e7 10 ♗xe7 ♔xe7 11 ♖d1 ♘f6 12 ♘e5 ♕d6 13 ♘c4 ♘e4 14 ♕c1 ♕c6 15 f3 ♘d6

16 ♕g5+?

16 ♘e5 or 16 e4 keeps the game balanced. The text-move falls into an ambush:

16...f6!

To his dismay, White discovers that after 17 ♕xg7+ ♘f7 the black knight keeps the lady in a cage. He will not be able to thwart both 18...♖ag8 and 18...♕xc4.

17 d5 ♕xc4 18 ♕xg7+ ♘f7 19 e4 ♕b3 20 dxe6 ♕xe6 21 ♖c1 c5

Black allows his rival to regain some material and simplifies into an advantageous ending.

22 ♗c4 ♖ag8 23 ♕xh8 ♕xc4 24 ♖xc4 ♖xh8 25 ♔f2 ♘e5 26 ♖c3 ♖d8 (0-1, 33 moves)**

Into the Lion's Den

Planting a piece in the heart of the opponent's formation frequently involves a serious risk; lacking support, the infiltrator might get caught.

Backemeyer – Meyer

German Bundesliga 2000

White to play

15 ♘e3 ♛a2?

Admittedly, Black's position is cheerless even after other moves; but the natural "threatening" text-move loses at once.

16 ♔d2! 1-0

The threat 17 ♖a1 leads to total collapse.

Kotov – A. Zaitsev

Sochi 1967

1 c4 f5 2 ♘c3 ♘f6 3 ♘f3 d6 4 d4 c6 5 ♗g5 ♘bd7 6 e3 e5 7 dxe5 dxe5 8 ♛c2 e4 9 ♘d4 ♘e5 10 0-0-0 ♛e7 11 f3! exf3 12 gxf3 ♛f7 13 f4 ♘xc4 14 ♗xc4 ♛xc4 15 ♗xf6 gxf6 16 ♘xf5?!

So far, White has dictated the course of events. His last move, though, offers Black, despite his shattered pawn structure and insecure king, some tactical chances. 16 e4! is stronger by far.

16...♛c5! 17 ♛e4+ ♔f7 18 ♖d8?! ♗xf5! 19 ♛e8+ ♔g7 20 ♖xa8

White has won the exchange and his queen and rook have penetrated Black's first rank. Nevertheless the upcoming rejoinder upsets the whole picture.

20...♔h6!!

Suddenly 21...♗g7 becomes an embarrassing threat to reckon with. The try 21 ♛d8!?, envisaging 21...♗g7 22 ♛d2! ♖xa8 23 e4 ♗xe4 24 f5+, fails to 21...♗e7!! 22 ♛xh8 ♛xe3+ 23 ♔d1 ♛f3+ 24 ♔d2 ♛g2+ with a winning attack.

21 ♖e1 ♗g7 22 ♛xh8 ♗xh8 23 ♖xh8 b5! 24 a3 a5 25 e4 ♛f2! 26 ♖e2 ♛xf4+ 27 ♖d2 ♗g6 28 b4 axb4 29 axb4 c5!

Black is in firm control. He went on to win on the 39th move.

Despite the grim experiences the infiltrators suffered in the two previous examples, they frequently reap positive rewards.

Bisguier – Fuderer

Interzonal, Gothenburg 1955

1 e4 c5 2 ♘f3 d6 3 g3 ♘f6 4 d3 b6 5 ♗g2 ♗b7 6 0-0 g6 7 ♘h4 ♘c6 8 f4 ♗g7 9 ♘d2 0-0 10 c3 ♘d7 11 a4? a6 12 f5 b5 13 axb5 axb5 14 ♖xa8 ♛xa8 15 fxg6 hxg6 16 ♘2f3 ♛a2! 17 ♖f2 ♛b1

Having penetrated deep into the enemy camp, the black queen makes it difficult for White to manoeuvre.

18 ♘d2

18 ♕c2 ♕a1 19 ♖f1 is more tenacious.

18...♕a1

Not 18...♕xd3? 19 ♖f3. But White's weaknesses in the centre and on the queenside must soon tell.

19 ♕c2 ♘7e5 20 ♗f1 ♘g4 21 ♖e2 b4 22 ♘b3 ♕a7 23 c4 ♕a4! 24 ♘f3 ♖a8 25 ♗g5 ♗c8 26 ♖e1 ♘5e5 27 ♘xe5 ♗xe5 28 ♖a1? ♕xb3! 0-1

After 29 ♕xb3 ♖xa1 White can choose between 30 ♕c2 ♗h3 or the equally distressing 30 ♔g2 ♘d4.

Lagvilava – Lacos

Tel-Aviv 2001

White to play

White would like to increase the pressure against the weak f7 pawn. Ideally he would install his white-squared bishop on d5, but in the diagrammed position this is impractical. So how about targeting f7 from the rear?

22 ♗h3! ♖f6 23 ♗d7 ♘d8 24 ♕d5 ♖xf1+ 25 ♖xf1 ♗g7

25...♗f6? 26 ♗c5. But now the white bishop achieves its aim.

26 ♗e8! ♕c7

26...♕e6? 27 ♗xf7+.

27 ♗d6 ♕c2 28 ♗xf7+ ♔h8 29 ♗e5 ♕xd3 30 ♗xg6! ♕xf1+

Desperation. 30...hxg6 loses to 31 ♖f8+ ♔h7 32 ♕g8+.

31 ♔xf1 hxg6 32 ♗xg7+ ♔xg7 33 ♕xd4+ 1-0

When many pieces infiltrate into the opponent's domain, the infiltrator's chances of success increase. The more forces that invade enemy territory, the more support they lend each other.

Shmuter – Afek

Israeli cup 1995

1 e4 c5 2 ♘f3 ♘c6 3 d4 cxd4 4 ♘xd4 ♘f6 5 ♘c3 g6 6 ♘xc6 bxc6 7 e5 ♘g8

This variation has a dubious reputation. Black's last move is forced, as 7...♘d5? leads to disaster after 8 ♘xd5 cxd5 9 ♕xd5 ♖b8 10 e6! fxe6? 11 ♕e5, forking both rooks.

8 ♗c4 ♗g7 9 ♗f4 ♕a5 10 0-0 ♗xe5 11 ♗xe5 ♕xe5 12 ♖e1 ♕g7 13 ♕d6 ♕f6 14 ♕c7 ♔f8 15 ♘d5! ♕d4 16 ♕d8+ ♔g7 17 ♘c7 ♕b6

If Black pinned his hopes on this pin *(sic.)* he is in for a big shock:

18 ♗xf7! ♘h6

On 18...♔xf7? comes 19 ♕e8+ ♔g7 20 ♘xa8 ♕b8 21 ♖e3 ♕xa8 22 ♖f3, winning. Black is now hoping for 19 ♘e8+ ♖xe8 20 ♕xe8 e6! But White has something better up his sleeve:

19 ♗e8!!

Astonishingly, White acquiesces to a second self-pin!

19...♘f5 20 ♖xe7+! ♔h6

20...♘xe7 21 ♕xe7+ followed by 22 ♘xa8.

21 ♖e5 ♗b7

What else? 21...♕d4 (21...♕xb2 22 ♖ae1) 22 ♖xf5! gxf5 23 ♘e6! is crushing.

22 ♕xd7 ♖c8 23 ♘e6 1-0

Capturing the Weaker Piece

In many positions we are faced with a choice of capturing more than one enemy piece. As a rule, we choose to capture the stronger piece. Exceptions evoke surprise.

Socko – Inkariev

Skanska open 2004

White to play

The ♗g5 is in an awkward position due to the threat of 19...h6.

19 ♗f1 h6 20 ♕h5 ♘xf4!! 21 ♕xe8 hxg5

Amazingly, the queen has no refuge. Materially, White is doing fine, but the positional advantage is firmly in Black's hands. After 22 ♕xa8 ♖xa8 Black will plant a strong knight on d3.

22 ♕e7 ♗f6 23 ♕xd7 ♘xd7 24 ♘b5 ♘c5 25 ♘xc7 ♖ac8 26 ♘b5 ♗e5 27 ♖cd1 ♘fd3 28 ♗xd3 ♘xd3

29 ♖f1 ♗f4 30 ♘c2 ♔h7 31 ♘cd4 ♗e3+ 32 ♔h2 ♗xd4 33 ♘xd4 ♔g6 34 g3?! ♖f7 35 ♘e6 ♖h7 36 h4 gxh4 37 ♘f4+ ♘xf4 38 gxf4 ♔f6 39 ♖g1 ♖e8 40 ♖g5 e3 41 ♖dg1 ♖h6 42 ♖e1 ♖g6 (0-1, 55 moves).

Bilek – Tal

Moscow 1967

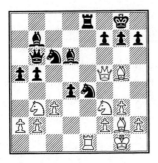

Black to play

20...♘e7 21 ♗xe7?

An error in a critical position. 21 ♖xe4! ♘xf5 22 ♖xe8+ ♗f8 23 ♘e5! leads to an advantage for White. A later game, Katona – Skorpik, corr. 1973-75, went: 23...♕c7 24 ♗d8! ♕c8 (24...♕d6

25 ♘xd4 ♘xd4 26 cxd4 ♗xg2 27 ♗e7 winning) 25 ♗xb7 ♕xb7 26 ♘c5 dxc3 27 ♘ed7 h6 28 ♘xb7 cxb2 29 ♖e1 ♘d4 30 ♖b1 ♗a3 31 ♗xa5 1-0

21...g6! 22 ♕h3 dxc3! 23 ♖xe4

23 ♗xd6 ♕xf2+ 24 ♔h1 ♕xe1+ 25 ♘xe1 ♘f2+ 26 ♔g1 ♘xh3+ 27 ♗xh3 ♖xe1+ 28 ♔f2 cxb2 29 ♘d2 ♖d1 and wins.

23...cxb2!

Once again, Black prefers to capture a pawn, not an officer. 23...♗xe4? 24 ♘g5 h5 25 ♗xd6 ♗xg2 26 ♕d7! is good for White.

Now 24 ♕h6 b1=♕+ 25 ♗f1 ♕xe4 26 ♘g5? is countered by 26...♕h1 mate.

24 ♖e1 ♖xe7 25 ♖b1 a4 26 ♘bd4

26 ♖xb2 axb3 27 axb3 is tougher, although Black remains on top.

26...♗xf3 27 ♘xf3 ♖e2! 28 ♖f1

28 ♕c8+ ♔g7 29 ♕c3+ ♗e5 is curtains.

28...♖xf2! 29 ♕c8+ ♔g7 30 ♕c3+ f6 0-1

Part Two:

Principled Issues Concerning 'Devious Chess'

Having acquainted ourselves with the characteristics of 'devious chess' in Part One, we move on to Part Two, which revolves around some of its central issues.

Chapter 6 argues that the complexity we experience in 'devious chess' derives from the need to approach certain positions in a different way from which we analyze and evaluate common positions.

Chapter 7 presents the dilemma we encounter when it is not clear whether our opponent's move is an error or a trap. Distinguishing between the two is usually easy: proof can be obtained through analysis. In complex positions, however, such proof may be elusive.

In the next two chapters, 8 and 9, we examine methods of handling unconventional chess from both sides of the board: we get to know the initiator's point of view and also the perspective of his counterpart.

Chapter Six:

Twists and Turns

The majority of positions that evolve during a chess game are characterized by the following mechanism: a player conceives an idea; he checks it; and then concludes whether or not it is viable.

If the move or plan is evaluated as good, he pursues it; but if he believes that the opponent has a strong antidote, he forsakes the idea and switches his attention to other directions.

Of course, there are variations to this theme. For instance, a wrong plan may be pursued because the refutation is missed.

Grinberg – Cuelliar

Israeli championship 1980

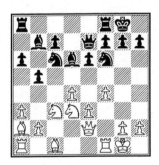

White to play

White sought to increase his space advantage by **14 e4?**

The threat 15 e5 seems deadly.

14...♘xd4 15 ♕f2

Expecting 15...e5? 16 fxe5 ♗xe5 17 ♘xe5 ♕xe5 18 ♗f4 ♕c5 19 ♗e3.

15...♘g4!

The refutation. 16 ♕xd4 loses to 16...c5, when the queen is amusingly trapped.

16 ♕g3 ♗xe4! 17 ♔h1 ♗xd3 18 ♕xd3 ♕h4 (0-1, 38 moves).

Sometimes the refutation is imaginary, and exists only in the player's mind; at other times, it has a solid objective basis.

On many occasions the idea seems to be playable, is implemented successfully in the game, and a rebuttal is found only in the *post mortem.*

In the following example, a refutation was found 30 years after the game, with computer assistance. [15]

Berkovitch – Nagar

Israeli championship
(quarter finals) 1967

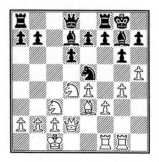

Black to play

14...♘c4 15 ♕e2 ♘xe3 16 ♕xe3 ♕b6

In addition to the crude 17...♕(♗)xd4, Black threatens 17...e5.

17 ♖d1 e5 18 ♘d5 exd4 19 ♘xb6 dxe3 20 ♘xd7 e2 21 ♖xd6

21 ♖de1 ♖fd8.

21...♗h6+ 22 ♔b1 ♗f4! 23 ♖d3 ♗g3 24 hxg6 hxg6 25 ♘xf8 ♔xf8 26 c4

Or 26 ♖e3 ♗f2!, when Black wins material and the game.

26...e1=♕+ 27 ♖xe1 ♗xe1 (0-1, 41 moves).

Only recently has it transpired that instead of 18 ♘d5, White could have turned the tables with **18 ♘f5!!**.

After 18...gxf5 (18...♕xe3+ 19 ♘xe3 leads to a clear edge for White) 19 ♕xb6 axb6 20 gxf5 we reach the following intriguing position:

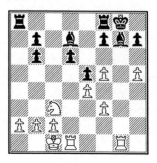

(variation)

Black to play

White regains his material losses, remaining with a large advantage: 20...♔h8 (forced) 21 ♖xd6 (double threat) ♖fd8 (double defence) 22 ♖gd1, etc.; 21...♖g8, intending 22...♗h6+ is the lesser evil, but then 22 ♖xg7 with 23 ♖xd7 still favours White.

* * * *

There are positions, though, that deviate from the basic idea-refutation pattern, and demand a more subtle treatment. These positions contain additional ingredients.

Let us begin with two simple illustrations.

Toshkov – Russek

Saint John 1988

White to play

1 e5 is an interesting idea, with the double threat 2 exd6(f6) and 2 ♕xg6. Black can defend with **1...♘xe5** which seems to foil White's plots. However, a new idea comes in handy – **2 f4!** and the knight is trapped in mid-board. Hence, the 'refutation' is countered by a 'counter- refutation'.

Schon – Hellers

Berlin 1988

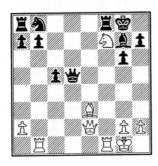

White to play

If White could dislodge the black queen from the a2-g8 diagonal, he would quickly achieve victory by ♕e2-c4.

22 ♖bd1 ♕e4 23 ♘g5 ♖xf1+ 24 ♖xf1 ♕xe3+!

24...♕d5 25 ♖d1, or 24...♕a4 25 ♕f3 is hopeless. The text move seems to save Black, but is defeated by a neat counter-stroke.

25 ♕xe3 ♗d4 26 ♖f8+! 1-0

We argue that in certain positions the struggle of idea versus refutation is prolonged and develops into a repeated procedure: idea – refutation – counter-refutation – counter-counter-refutation, and so on.

Let us look at some examples.

Hodakowsky – Heinrich

West German championship 1957

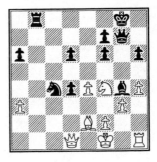

White to play

Black has a concrete threat: 23...♖b1! 24 ♕xb1 ♘d2+. It is likely that White's first thoughts were directed to thwart this malice. The simple 23 ♔g2 or 23 ♕xd4 are natural and strong.

But then, a fresh idea cropped up: why not allow Black to execute his plan, garnering more than sufficient compensation for the queen?

23 ♗xg4! ♖b1 24 ♕xb1 ♘d2+ 25 ♔g2 ♘xb1 26 ♘h5!

The point. 26...♕xg4 fails to 27 ♘xf6+, and otherwise White will continue 27 ♖xb1, winning on material.

26...♕g6

Is this a refutation? 27 ♖xb1 falls short to 27...♕xe4+ with 28...♕xb1.

27 ♗f5! ♕xh5 28 g4

A counter-refutation.

28...♕xf5 29 exf5 ♘xa3

Or 29...♘c3 30 ♖h3.

30 ♖a1 ♘c4 31 ♖a4 (1-0, 41 moves)

Panczuk – Matlak

Polish championship 1992

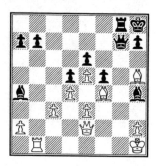

Black to play

1...♗b5!

A tempting, aesthetically-pleasing move, threatening to invade decisively with 2...♗d3-e4. The bishop is taboo: 2 ♖xb5 ♕g1 mate; 2 ♕xb5 ♕g2 mate.

2 ♗h6!

A counter stroke. 2...♗xe2 allows 3 ♗xg7+, while 2...♕xh6 is met by 3 ♖xb5.

2...♕g6!

A counter-counter-refutation. The ♗b5 is still untouchable, while 3 ♗xg6? loses to 3...♗xe2.

3 ♕f3

For the time being, everything is defended.

3...♗d3

This also had to be foreseen in advance.

4 ♗xg6 ♗xb1 5 ♗f7 ♗e4 6 ♕xe4 fxe4

Black stays ahead on material, since 7 ♗xg8 ♔xg8 leads to a winning bishop-ending for Black (♗h4-e1-xc3).

7 ♗f4 ♗f2 8 h3 ♖g6! 9 ♗xg6 hxg6 10 ♔g2 ♗e1 and Black won. Meyer and Muller [16] point out that 8 h4! affords White real chances of salvation (8...♖g6 9 h5!); but this is outside our discussion.

Golovko – Averbach

Moscow championship 1950

Black to play

Averbach launches a complex combination:

20...♗a4! 21 b3 ♗xb3 22 ♕xb3 ♖a3

The idea: Black appears to regain his piece with interest.

23 ♕c4 ♖xf3 24 ♕g4

Is this a refutation? The fork of rook and knight seems to leave White on top.

24...♖d3! 25 ♕xd7

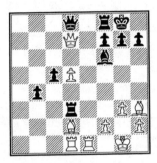

25...♖xd5! 26 ♕xd8 ♖fxd8

A counter-refutation. Admittedly, Black has no immediate threat because of the vulnerability of his first rank; but after making *luft* with, say, 27...g6, the pin on the d-file nets Black material. 27 ♗g4, defending d1, (counter-counter-refutation?) is met by 27...h5! (counter-counter-counter-refutation!).

27 ♗g2 ♖d3 28 ♗f1 ♖3d4 29 ♗xb4 ♖xd1 30 ♖xd1 ♖xd1 (0-1, 57 moves)

The continuous struggle between ideas and counter-ideas is frequently seen in studies.

G. Nadariashvili

Revista de Sah 1973

White to play and draw

1 ♖d4

The first idea – preventing Black from promoting to a queen. 1...d1=♕+ 2 ♖xd1 ♘xd1 3 ♗e1 draws.

1...♘f5

A counter-idea – forking two pieces. Black hopes to win material after 2 ♖d5 ♘xg3 3 ♔b3 ♘f1.

2 ♗f4! ♘xd4 3 ♗xd2!

A fresh twist, aiming at stalemate (3...♗xd2?=).

3...♘b3!!

A brilliant riposte. If 4 ♗xc1 then 4...♘c5 mate! (but not the meek 4...♘xc1? stalemate).

4 ♗b4!!

Yet another twist. The threat 5 ♔xb3 forces matters.

4...axb4 5 axb4 ♘ moves Stalemate!

Back to practical chess – and to another example of a see-saw kind of game:

Arizmendi – Milov

Biel 2001

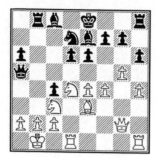

White to play

19 ♘c6!!

An exceptional idea, all the more so since its 'refutation' is apparently so obvious:

19...♕xc3

What now? 20 ♘xb8? ♕xe3; or 20 ♗d4 ♖xb2+ 21 ♔c1 ♖xc2+ 22 ♕xc2 ♕xc2+ 23 ♔xc2 ♗b7! are to Black's advantage.

20 ♗c1!

Threatening simply 21 ♘xb8. Meanwhile, the black queen has nowhere to go.

20...♖b6 21 ♔a1!

21 ♖h3? ♕xh3 22 ♕xh3 ♖xc6 is unsatisfactory. Now the sly 21...♗f6?! fails against 22 e5!.

21...♕xc2 22 ♕xc2 ♖xc6 23 ♗d2 h5 24 ♗b4 a5 25 ♗xa5 0-0 26 ♗b4 e5 27 f5 ♗b7 28 f6 gxf6 29 ♕e2 ♖b6 30 ♖dg1 f5 31 ♕xh5 ♖a8 32 g6 1-0

The next position is one of the most remarkable I have ever seen. The evaluation changes time and again and it is difficult to assert where, in essence, is the final "end-point" of it.

Mor – Mart

Israel 1969

Black to play

In the diagram position, Black could have played **1...♕xh2 2 ♕xb5** (otherwise Black is simply a pawn up) **2...♕h4+**, which opens the gate to some fascinating developments. We follow the analysis of Uri Avner, a renowned problemist and analyst. His conclusions, made shortly after the game, have withstood the test of time. [17]

3 ♔e2 (apparently forced) **♖xe3+! 4 ♔xe3 ♗d4+!!**

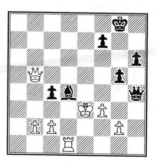

(variation)

Splendid. Mate is forced: 5 ♖xd4 ♕e1 mate; or 5 ♔e2 ♕f2 mate; or 5 ♔d2 ♕f4+ 6 ♔e2 ♕e3+ 7 ♔f1 ♕f2 mate.

But White can improve with **3 ♔f1! ♖xe3 4 ♖d8+ ♗f8** (4...♔h7?? 5 ♕f5 mate) **5 ♕b4!** – preventing mate on e1 and menacing f8.

But this is definitely not the end! Black responds with **5...♔h7! 6 ♖xf8 ♕d4!!**, when White faces insurmountable difficulties.

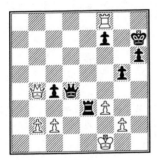

(variation)

The main threat is 7...♕d1+ 8 ♔f2 ♖e2+ 9 ♔g3 ♕d4! (switchback) with unavoidable mate.

7 ♖xf7+ ♔g6 8 ♖b7!

Not 8 ♖e7 ♕d1+ 9 ♔f2 ♕e2+, winning a rook. Now another re-evaluation is called for: after 8...♕d1+ 9 ♔f2 ♖e2+ 10 ♔g3 ♕d4 White is saved by 11 ♕b6+. But...

8...♔h5!!

Avoids the saving check at the end of the previous variation. Now White is really helpless.

Su. Polgar – Chiburdanidze

Olympiad, Calvia 2004

1 ♘f3 ♘f6 2 c4 e6 3 ♘c3 ♗b4 4 ♕c2 0-0 5 a3 ♗xc3 6 ♕xc3 c5 7 b4 b6 8 ♗b2 d6 9 g4!?

In a way, this move burns the bridges; neither king will find a safe haven.

9...♗b7 10 g5 ♘h5 11 ♖g1 e5 12 ♗h3 ♘f4 13 ♗f5

A sacrifice of the knight on e5 is in the offing. However, the immediate 13 ♘xe5? dxe5 14 ♕xe5 is countered by 14...♘d3+! 15 exd3 ♖e8.

13...g6?

13...♘c6 is simple and healthy. Of course, the ex lady world champion with the black pieces realized that she was inviting the ensuing sacrifice, but thought she would have the last laugh.

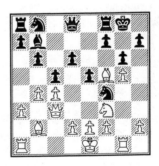

14 ♘xe5!

Apparently, a straight refutation of Black's move. 14...gxf5? 15 ♘c6 is plain sailing, while after 14...dxe5? 15 ♕xe5, White regains the piece with interest. Similarly, 14...♕e7!? fails to 15 ♗e4!! ♗xe4 (15...dxe5

16 ♗xb7 ♕xb7 17 ♕xe5) 16 ♘c6 ♘d3+ 17 ♔f1 and White wins.

Nor does 14...♕e8 help, because of 15 ♗e4! ♗xe4 16 ♘g4 f6 17 ♘h6+ ♔g7 18 gxf6+ ♔xh6 19 ♕g3!.

14...♘xe2!

A counter blow: 15 ♔xe2? dxe5 and White cannot capture on e5 on account of ...♖e8.

15 ♘xf7!!

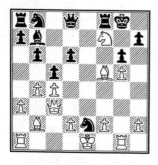

It transpires that Black is the victim, rather than the hunter, of this stunning sequence: 15...♖xf7? 16 ♕h8 mate; 15...♔xf7? 16 ♕g7+ ♔e8 17 ♗f6! wins.

15...♘xc3 16 ♘h6+ ♔g7 17 ♗xc3+ ♖f6 18 ♗xf6+ ♕xf6 19 gxf6+ ♔xh6

The fog has cleared and White is left with a winning advantage. 20 ♖c1!, intending ♖c3-h3, is immediately decisive. White's actual choice, although slower, collects the point nonetheless.

20 ♗e6 ♘c6 21 ♗d5 ♖f8 22 f7 ♘d8 23 ♗xb7 ♘xb7 24 ♖g3 ♖xf7 25 ♖e3 ♘d8 26 b5 (1-0, 39 moves).

Not infrequently one can see players missing their way in complicated positions. A common source of error is halting calculations too soon.

Uhlmann – Hennings

East Germany 1968

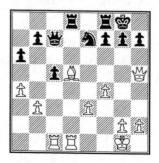

White to play

White played 1 ♗f3?, eventually winning, after Black misplayed his chances.

Uhlmann contemplated **1 ♖xc5 ♕xc5 2 ♗xf7+** but concluded that after **2...♔h8 3 ♕xc5** (3 ♖xd8?? ♕xe3+) **♖xd1+ 4 ♔f2 ♖xf7**, Black's material compensation outweighed the gain of a queen.

Had he looked one move further, he might have found a counter-counter-refutation: **5 ♕h5!!**

The fork wins a whole rook: **5...♖d2+ 6 ♔e1 g6 7 ♕e5+.**

* * * *

Is there a practical lesson to be drawn from these examples?

I suggest that when players encounter a position of the "twists and turns" type, they tend to react in one of two principal ways. Some will make a determined effort to get to the bottom of things, to discover the ultimate truth. But many more will refrain from entering such positions altogether, being unable to handle the uncertainty and ambiguity involved. Identifying where to stop calculating is frequently a most difficult task.

Szabo – Czerniak

Olympiad, Moscow 1956

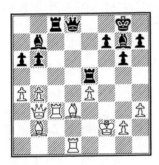

Black to play

Black deliberated here a long time, analyzing the consequences of **22...♕d4+ 23 ♔f1 ♖f5+!! 24 exf5 ♕f4+ 25 ♔g1** (or 25 ♔e1 ♗xc3+ 26 ♗xc3 ♖e8+ 27 ♗e2 ♗xg2 with a vicious attack) **♗d4+ 26 ♔h1 ♗xg2+?! 27 ♔xg2 ♕f2+ 28 ♔h1 ♕f3+**; but he was not convinced that the resulting position offered more than perpetual check. [18] [We shall just mention that en route Black missed the vastly superior 26...♖xc3 – since 27 ♗xc3 ♕g3 is futile].

In the end Black abandoned the line altogether and opted for 22...♕h4+?

23 ♔g1 ♖ce8. Later on he went astray and lost in 31 moves.

Returning to the position after 28...♕f3+, it was later revealed that Black *did* have a win: **29 ♔h2 ♗e5+ 30 ♔g1 ♕g3+ 31 ♔f1 ♕xh3+ 32 ♔e2 ♕g2+ 33 ♔e3 ♖e8!!** (a quite, deadly move) **34 ♖c8!** (a refutation?) **34...♗f4++!!** (no!)

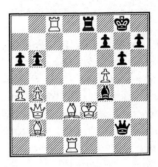

White is mated, e.g. 35 ♔d4 (35 ♔xf4 g5 mate) ♕f2+ 36 ♔d5 ♕f3+ 37 ♔d4 ♗e5+ 38 ♔c4 ♖xc8 mate.

Chess players tend to complain when they get a routine type of position. "Boring" – they grumble – "If only I had an interesting position...". Yet, given a choice, many of them often steer the game towards standard, well-known set-ups, on top of the murky Mor-Mart type of position, analyzed previously.

Even a courageous, imaginative player like Mikhail Tal shied away from the storm when his opponent, as Black, provoked him after **1 e4 ♘f6 2 e5 ♘d5 3 d4 d6 4 ♘f3 dxe5 5 ♘xe5** with the strange **5...♘d7?!**

Tal – Larsen

Candidates match, Bled 1965

Tal testifies that he pondered the consequences of 6 ♘xf7 ♔xf7 7 ♕h5+ ♔e6 8 c4 ♘5f6 9 d5+ ♔d6 10 ♕f7 ♘e5 11 ♗f4, for 50 minutes. *"In one of the innumerable variations I found something resembling a defence, and (I) rejected the sacrifice"* [19] – something he lamented for years.

* * * *

Here are some tricky positions to challenge the readers. One piece of advice: whenever you feel that you've reached a clear verdict, think again: look out for counter-counter-counter-refutations!

-1-

Gamback – Dotschew

Greece 2001

1 e4 e6 2 d4 d5 3 ♘d2 c5 4 c3 cxd4 5 cxd4 dxe4 6 ♘xe4 ♗d7 7 ♘f3 ♗c6 8 ♗d3 ♘f6 9 ♘xf6+ ♕xf6?!

We can assume that Black was familiar with the basic tactical motive 10 ♗g5 ♗xf3 11 ♕d2 ♕xd4 12 ♗b5+; but he had prepared a counter-stroke. Who will have the last laugh?

-2-

Janowsky – Burn

Cologne 1898

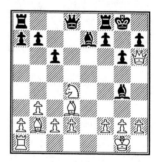

Black to play

White is the exchange down, but maintains a strong initiative: 19 ♕g7+!! ♔xg7 20 ♘f5++ ♔g8 21 ♘h6 mate is one of several threats. The natural defence, 18...♗f6, is countered by 19 ♕f4!, intending both 20 ♕xg4 and 20 ♘xc6

18...♗g5

This looks like a gross oversight, on account of **19 ♘f5.** Is it?

-3-

Dorfman – Thorsteins

New-York 1989

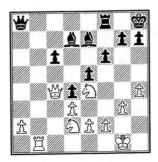

Black to play

Black tried to expand the scope of his cramped pieces with **23...c5.** It seems quite dangerous to capture this pawn, but GM Dorfman is not faint-hearted and after deliberation accepted the challenge.

24 ♘xc5

Now 24...♖c8? fails to 25 ♘xd7 ♖xc4 26 ♘xc4, coupled with 27 ♖b8. So Black chose:

24...♗h3

White can defend with 25 f3 but after 25...♗xc5 26 ♕xc5 ♖c8 Black regains his pawn. Instead, Dorfman opted for

25 ♖b7

A brave move indeed, but is it correct?

-4-

Edwards – Guillot

Correspondence, USA 1990

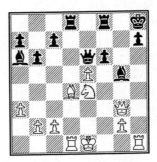

Black to play

A series of best moves for both sides led to a crazy position.

Chapter Seven:

The Trap vs. Blunder Dilemma

One of the common dilemmas faced by players occurs when our opponent makes a move which appears to be a serious mistake: it jettisons material, falls into our plans, or simply contradicts common sense.

On the one hand – if the opponent *did* make a mistake, it is a cause for celebration. On the other hand, our interpretation might be erroneous: the ostensible blunder may prove to have been an ambush.

Marjanovic – Gunawan

Jakarta 1986

1 e4 e5 2 ♘f3 ♘c6 3 ♗b5 a6
4 ♗a4 ♘f6 5 d4 exd4 6 0-0 ♗e7 7 e5
♘e4 8 ♘xd4 ♘xd4 9 ♕xd4 ♘c5
10 ♘c3 0-0 11 ♗g5 ♘xa4 12 ♗xe7

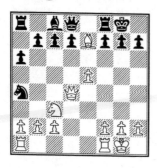

Now the simple 12...♕xe7 is indicated; but Black assumed that

White had missed something in his calculations:

12...♘xc3?

The continuations 13 ♗xd8 ♘e2+, and 13 ♕xc3 ♕xe7 leave Black a piece ahead.

13 ♕h4!! 1-0

After 13...♘e2+ 14 ♔h1 ♕e8 15 ♗xf8 ♕xf8 16 ♖ae1 Black ends up the exchange down, with no counterplay.

Frequently a thin line separates a trap from a blunder. After **1 e4 c5 2 ♘f3 d6 3 c3 ♘f6** we reach the following position.

Black's last move does not contain a threat. After, say, **4 ♗e2, 4...♘xe4?** is a blunder on account of 5 ♕a4+, grabbing the knight.

But then, there are nuances:

After **1 e4 c5 2 ♘f3 d6 3 c3 ♘f6 4 h3 ♘c6 5 d4? cxd4 6 cxd4** Black may safely capture on e4, since **6...♘xe4 7 d5** (intending to check on a4 if ♘c6 moves) is met by **7...♛a5+** (this possibility was missed by Partos in his game vs. Ljubojevic, Interzonal, Biel 1985).

Or: **1 e4 c5 2 ♘e2 d6 3 c3 ♘f6 4 g3? ♘xe4! 5 ♛a4+ ♗d7 6 ♛xe4 ♗c6 7 ♛e3 ♗xh1 8 f3** and now, instead of 8...g5? 9 g4 h5 10 ♘g3 hxg4 11 ♘xh1 (Ermenkov – Hmadi, Interzonal, Tunis 1985), Black could gain the upper hand by 8...♘c6-e5.

Another variation on the same theme: **1 e4 e5 2 f4 d5 3 exd5 e4 4 d3 ♘f6 5 dxe4 ♘xe4 6 ♘f3**. Now **6...♗b4+??** (Tagnon – Jojic, Paris 1985) is a grave error: **7 c3** and withdrawing the ♗b4 allows 8 ♛a4+ while 7...♛e7 8 ♛a4+ ♗d7 9 ♛xb4 is also of little help.

However, after the sequence **1 e4 ♘f6 2 ♘c3 d5 3 e5 ♘e4 4 ♘ce2 d4 5 c3**, the move **5...dxc3** is not a blunder, since the apparently lethal **6 ♛a4+**

is countered by **6...♘d7!** (and not...**resigns**, as in Grondechevsky – Ohlin, Moscow 1973!) **7 ♛xe4?**

(7 dxc3) ♘c5, when Black regains material and is better off.

Livshin – Liberzon

Moscow 1955

1 ♘f3 ♘f6 2 g3 e6 3 ♗g2 d5 4 c4 ♗e7 5 0-0 0-0 6 b3 c5 7 ♗b2 ♘c6 8 cxd5 exd5 9 d4 ♘e4 10 dxc5?! ♗xc5 11 ♘c3 ♘xc3 12 ♗xc3 d4 13 ♗b2 ♗f5 14 ♖c1 ♗b6 15 ♛d2

White intends 16 ♖fd1, exerting pressure against Black's isolated pawn. 15...♛d7, coupled with 16...♖fd8, is natural, but Black chooses a different path.

15...♗e4 16 ♖fd1 ♛d5

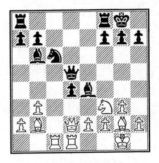

Now White embarks on a tactical scheme, designed to free his position.

17 ♘xd4?!

Did Black miss it? After 17...♗xg2 18 ♘xc6 bxc6 White has 19 ♛c3!, with an embarrassing double threat.

17...♗xd4 18 ♗xe4 ♛xe4!

Black can get his pawn back by 18...♗xf2+ 19 ♔xf2 ♛xe4; but after 20 ♛g5 ♛g6 21 ♛xg6, his winning chances are meagre.

19 ♗xd4 ♖ad8 20 e3

Relatively better is 20 ♖xc6, trying to hold the endgame with a pawn for the exchange.

20...♘e5

Now it is obvious that winning a pawn was not a profitable deal. The weakness of the light-coloured squares around the white king is irreparable; the rest is agony.

21 ♕c2 ♘f3+ 22 ♔h1 ♕g4 23 ♕e2 ♖d5 24 ♖c5 ♖d6 25 ♔g2 ♖h6 26 ♖h1 ♘h4+ 27 ♔f1 ♕e4 28 f3 ♘xf3 29 ♕c2 ♕g4 30 ♕f5 ♘xh2+ 31 ♔f2 b6 32 ♖d5 ♖c8 33 ♖d1 ♕xf5+ 34 ♖xf5 g6 35 ♖f4 f5 36 ♔e2 ♘g4 37 e4 ♖h2+ 38 ♔f3 ♖c3+! 0-1

Hodge – Jens

Junior Team Tournament, Bruges 1999

White to play

1 ♘b3!?

A shocking move. One reason Black delays the exchange ...cxd4 in this French formation is to prevent this very move. On the face of it, therefore, White's move has an air of a blunder about it.

1...c4 2 ♗xc4 dxc4 3 ♘bd2

White exploits the fact that Black's dark-squared bishop is temporarily distant and unable to cover the key-square d6. Still, it is unclear if the sacrifice is sound.

3...♕a6 4 ♘e4 ♘d8

Beliavsky & Mikhalchishin [21] treat White's play as an example of a valid intuitive sacrifice. We are not so convinced; 4...♘cxe5 5 dxe5 ♘xe5 6 ♘d6+ ♔f8 is a probable improvement.

5 ♘d6+ ♔e7

5...♔f8 seems better.

6 ♗g5+ f6 7 ♘h4! ♘f8 8 ♗h6 fxe5 9 dxe5 ♘f7 10 ♗xf8+ ♔xf8 11 ♕f3 1-0

The interpretation of one's opponent's moves is crucial: if we assess his moves as weak, we feel an urge to punish our rival, to refute his plans, to pursue victory. But when we consider our opponent's moves as dangerous, our vigilance increases, we contemplate our moves longer, checking and rechecking calculations.

Geller – Stean

Teesside 1975

1 ♘f3 c5 2 c4 g6 3 d4 cxd4 4 ♘xd4 ♘c6 5 e4 ♘f6 6 ♘c3 d6 7 ♗e2 ♘xd4 8 ♕xd4 ♗g7 9 ♗g5 ♗e6 10 ♖c1 ♕a5 11 ♕d2 ♖c8 12 f3!?

Ignoring Black's threat (12 b3 is natural and good). Can Black accept the gift?

GM McDonald observes that many players would be loath to accept a 'fishy' sacrifice against a strong attacking player, *"even if they couldn't foresee any evil consequence"*. [22] Playing safe is an option, of course, but what if accepting the pawn is a golden chance to upset the famous GM?

12...♗xc4

Stean decides not to take the word of his esteemed rival.

13 ♘d5 ♕xa2

Forced. 13...♕xd2+ 14 ♗xd2 loses material. The text move is aimed against 14 ♘b4 ♕b3 15 ♗d1 ♘xe4! when Black is OK.

14 0-0!?

14 ♘b4 is nevertheless the correct move, only after 14...♕b3 White should continue 15 e5! (instead of

15 ♗d1) ♘e4 16 fxe4 ♗xe5 17 0-0 with a considerable advantage. 14 ♘xe7!? ♔xe7 15 e5 is another interesting option.

14...♘xd5 15 ♖xc4!

15 ♗xc4 ♖xc4 16 ♕xd5 fails to 16...♗d4+ 17 ♔h1 ♖xc1!.

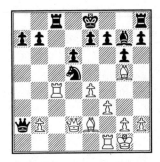

15...♖xc4?

This loses prettily. Best was 15...♘b6! 16 ♖xc8+ ♘xc8 17 ♗b5+ ♔d8! (17...♔f8 18 ♖c1 ♘b6 19 ♖c7 ♕xb2 20 ♗xe7+ ♔g8 21 ♕xb2 ♗xb2 21 ♖xb7 with an advantageous endgame).

Now Geller, in his original notes in *Chess* magazine, writes that 17...♔d8 is "completely bad" and gives 18 ♖c1 ♕xb2 19 ♕a5+ b6 20 ♕a6. [23] But if we continue with 20...♗d4+ 21 ♔h1 ♗c5 22 ♗c6 ♕e5 23 ♕b7 ♕e6, things are not so simple.

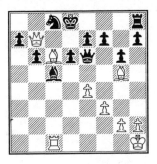

(variation)

Still Black is in a sort of zugzwang, so it is doubtful whether his defences hold after 24 ♖xc5! dxc5 (24...bxc5? 25 ♗d2) 25 ♗f4 ♘d6 26 ♕xa7 ♕c8 27 ♕xb6+ ♕c7 28 ♕xc5.

16 ♕xd5 ♖a4 17 ♗b5+ ♔f8 18 ♖c1! 1-0

Without waiting for 18...♗d4+ 19 ♕xd4! ♖xd4 20 ♗h6+ ♔g8 21 ♖c8 mate.

Mistaken identification of 'traps' for 'blunders' occurs even in the highest ranks:

Anand – Kasparov

PCA world championship,
New York 1995

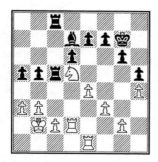

Black to play

27...♗e6?! 28 b4? axb4 (29) axb4 ♖c4

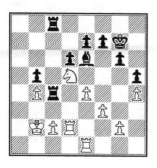

30 ♘b6?

Interviewed in *New in Chess* Kasparov remarked sarcastically: *"Before he played ♘b6 he spent less than one minute... (Couldn't) you think again? If you respect Kasparov, who is probably not that bad a player, do you think he missed losing an exchange?"* [24]

In this case, 27...♗e6 was a trap, not a blunder. 30 c3 ♗xd5 31 ♖xd5 ♖xc3 32 ♖e2 would retain drawing chances.

30...♖xb4+ 31 ♔a3 ♖xc2!! 0-1

32 ♖xc2 ♖b3+ 33 ♔a2 ♖e3+ is hopeless.

Here is another famous incident where a player misinterpreted a trap for a blunder.

Hübner – Adorjan

Match, Bad Lautenberg 1980

Black to play

61...♖a2+ 62 ♔f3

62 ♔h1 ♖c1+ would lose slowly; the text move sets a sly trap.

62...♖c3+ 63 ♔g4 ♖g2+ 64 ♔h5 ♖xg5+ 65 ♖xg5

Now 65...♖xh3 is easy; but why not liquidate into a simple pawn-endgame?

65...♖c5?? 66 ♔xh4! ♖xg5 Stalemate.

Indeed, the task of assessing correctly the meaning of the opponent's moves is sometimes so intricate that the instigator of the blunder/trap type of moves may also be baffled. The following two examples are lifted from an article I published in *Kingpin* magazine, under the heading "Winning by Blundering". [25] The initiator's original plans misfire, and salvation exists only by sheer luck.

Beni – Schwartzbach

Vienna 1969

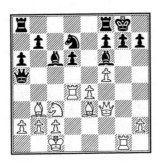

White to play

17 ♖xd6

After the game White revealed that he had conceived a grandiose idea:

17...♗xc3 18 bxc3 ♕xc3 19 ♗d4!! (The Windmill) ♕xf3 20 ♖xg7+ ♔h8 21 ♖xf7+ ♔g8 22 ♖g7+ with mate to follow.

17...♗xc3 18 bxc3 ♕a3+ 19 ♔b1 ♕xd6

Not quite as planned.

Deciding that there is always time to resign, White decided to hang on for a few more moves, only to discover, like magic, that he was winning!

20 ♗d4 ♕h6

Both 20...♘e5 21 ♕g3; and 20...g6 21 fxg6 hxg6 22 ♕h5 lose.

21 ♕h3!!

The Windmill is applied, nonetheless. The same idea can be accomplished with 21 ♕h5!!.

21...♕xh3 22 ♖xg7+ ♔h8 23 ♖xf7+ ♔g8 24 ♖g7+ ♔h8 25 ♖xd7+(?) 1-0

His last move misses a mate in one (25 ♖g8 mate) but is strong enough to force resignation.

Chandler – Leontxo Garcia

Alicante 1979

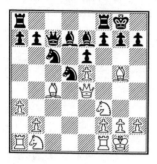

Black to play

13...♘xe5!?

Black reckons on 14 ♘xe5 ♗xg5, or 14 ♗xe7 ♘xf3+.

14 ♕xe5! ♕xc4 15 ♗xe7 ♘xe7 16 ♕d6

This was definitely not according to Black's plans when he played 13...♘xe5. A blunder, then?

Black now sank into deep thought and found a resource:

16...♘g6!

16...♗b5 17 ♘bd2.

17 ♕xd7 ♖fd8 18 ♕xb7

18 ♘bd2? ♕xf1+.

18...♖db8 ½-½

Drawn by repetition. Notice that had Black played 16...♘f5? instead of 16...♘g6, he would have lost to 19 ♕xf7+!.

In 'devious chess', the ability to distinguish accurately a trap from a blunder increases in importance.

Can you spot the difference between a blunder and a trap in the following set of positions?

-1-

Castaneda – W. Browne

World open, Philadelphia 1997

1 e4 c5 2 ♘f3 d6 3 d4 cxd4 4 ♘xd4 ♘f6 5 ♘c3 a6 6 ♗g5 e6 7 f4 ♘c6 8 ♘xc6 bxc6 9 e5 h6 10 ♗h4 g5 11 fxg5 ♘d5 12 ♘e4 ♕b6 13 ♗d3 hxg5 14 ♗xg5 ♖xh2

A temporary rook sacrifice (15 ♖xh2 ♕g1+). Is it sound?

-2-

Zalkind – Ribshtein

Israeli U-20 championship 1999

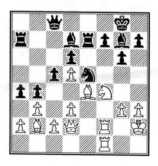

Black to play

41...♝h6

Literally begging for White's rejoinder:

42 ♘xg6

Your verdict, please.

-3-

Afek – Shirazi

St. Quentin 1999

1 e4 e5 2 ♘f3 ♘c6 3 ♘c3 ♘f6 4 d4 ♝b4 5 ♘xe5 ♕e7 6 ♕d3 ♘xe5 7 dxe5 ♕xe5 8 ♝d2 0-0 9 0-0-0 ♝xc3 10 ♝xc3 ♕f4+ 11 ♖d2 d5

Not 11...♘xe4? 12 ♕d4! f6 13 f3.

12 exd5 ♖e8 13 b3 ♘e4 14 ♕d4 ♕h6 15 ♝b5 c6 16 dxc6 bxc6 17 ♝xc6

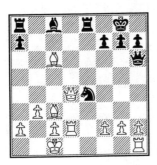

It is true that the bishop is 'taboo' as g7 must be guarded. On 17...♘xc3 comes 18 ♕xc3, not 18 ♝xe8?? ♘e2+.

But what is White to do against **17...♘xd2?**

-4-

Rubtsova – Belova

USSR 1945

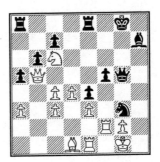

White to play

1 ♖f4

Intending 2 ♖g4, winning the queen.

1...♝g6

It seems that 2 ♖g4 is still extremely powerful. Was Black's last move a blunder?

-5-

Gumprich – Hennicke

Berlin 1931

White to play

The shaky position of the ♖d7 suggests **1 ♖fxf6**. Is it good?

Chapter Eight:
Methods of Conducting
'Devious Chess'

This chapter covers the basic patterns of unconventional chess. We shall accompany its practitioners *wreaking havoc* out of nowhere and infusing a packed dose of *confusion* to dormant situations. *Provoking* one's opponent and *complicating* the position are everyday tools in the realm of unconventional chess. *Opportunism* is not a coarse expression; striving to unsettle the game by *unbalancing the equilibrium* is a common routine; *desperate attacks* are recurrent weapons.

Setting Fire in the Desert

One criterion for assessing success is to measure the ratio between actions and the resources upon which they lean. Setting off explosions on the board when a player's whole army stands prepared is a frequent procedure. Creating tough problems for the opponent in a barren chess field is considerably harder.

How does one sift gold from sand? The familiar strategy is to continue battling without altering the situation, by building on the accumulation of minute advantages.

In the following two fragments, an 'unwinnable' position is transformed into victory by 'normal' means: the stronger and more experienced protagonist proceeds calmly, exploiting his rival's imprecisions to the full.

Thomson – Speelman

British championship 1992

Black to play

This ending is totally drawn. The pawn-structure on the queenside ensures that even if all kingside pawns are eliminated, White will be able to hold on. For instance, *White:* ♔d3, *Black:* ♔e5; White plays ♔c4, when ...♔e4 produces stalemate.

30...♔f6 31 ♔e2 ♔g5 32 ♔e3 f6 33 g3 hxg3 34 hxg3 g6 35 ♔e2 f5 36 ♔e3 ♔f6

36...f4+ 37 ♔f2=.

37 ♔d3

37 f4 seems to draw with ease.

37...f4 38 gxf4 exf4 39 ♔d4 g5 40 ♔c4 g4! 41 fxg4 ♔g5

Suddenly Black acquires substantial winning chances.

42 e5 f3 43 ♔d3 ♔xg4 44 e6 ♔g3 45 e7 f2 46 e8=♕

46 ♔e2 ♔g2 47 e8=♕ f1=♕+ 48 ♔d2 ♕f2+ 49 ♔e2 ♔g3! does not guarantee equality.

46...f1=♕+ 47 ♔c2 ♕f5+ 48 ♔b2 ♕f2+ 49 ♔b1 ♕g1+ 50 ♔a2 ♕f2+ 51 ♔b1 ♕xc5 52 ♕g6+ ♔f2 53 ♕f6+ ♔e2 54 ♕e6+ ♔d2 55 ♕h6+ ♕e3 56 ♕h2+ ♕e2 57 ♕f4+ ♔c3 0-1

Ivanchuk – Sutovsky

Copenhagen 2003

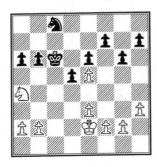

White to play

How is it possible for White to win? Even in retrospect, when one has witnessed the subsequent developments, there is no easy answer.

35 ♔d3 b5 36 ♘c3 ♘b6 37 f4 ♔c5 38 ♘e2 ♘c4 39 b3 ♘a3?

Black overestimates his chances on the queenside and will soon pay the price on the opposite wing.

40 ♘d4 b4 41 ♘f3! h6 42 ♘h2! ♘b5

Or 42...h5 43 ♘f3, and the knight is heading towards the hapless kingside black pawns.

43 ♘g4 ♘c3 44 ♘xh6 ♘xa2 45 ♘xf7 d4 46 ♘g5 dxe3 47 ♘xe6+ ♔c6 48 ♘d4+ ♔d5 49 ♘e2 a5 50 ♔xe3 1-0

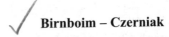

There is a different method of playing to win in positions which apparently hold no prospects. That is, to alter the situation dramatically: to infuse life into a corpse, to reignite a bloody fight out of the ashes.

Birnboim – Czerniak

Israeli championship 1976

1 d4 d5 2 c4 e6 3 ♘c3 c5 4 cxd5 cxd4 5 ♕xd4 ♘c6 6 ♕d1 exd5 7 ♕xd5 ♗e6 8 ♕xd8+ ♖xd8 9 ♗d2 ♘b4 10 ♖c1 ♘xa2 11 ♘xa2 ♗xa2 12 e4

12 ♖a1 ♗c4 13 ♖xa7? ♗a6.

12...a6 13 ♗c4 ♗xc4 14 ♖xc4 ♘e7 15 ♘e2 ♘c6 16 ♗c3 f6 17 ♘d4 ♘xd4 18 ♖xd4 ♖xd4 19 ♗xd4 ♗d6 20 ♔e2 ♔d7 21 ♖c1

Here Black must decide which endgame is more congenial for him: 21...♖e8 and 22...♗e5 leads to a rook-ending. In the game he prefers a bishop-ending. Both seem to be equal.

21...♖c8 22 ♖xc8 ♔xc8

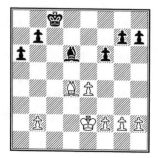

At this point we would expect the contestants to shake hands and split the point. But the game was played in the last round and in order to maintain his half-a-point lead over two of his rivals, Nathan Birnboim had to win. So he sharpened the battle, adopting an attitude of 'all or nothing'.

23 ♔e3 ♔d7 24 f4 a5 25 g4 b5 26 h4 a4 27 g5 ♔e6 28 f5+ ♔f7 29 h5 fxg5 30 e5 ♗b4 31 e6+ ♔f8 32 h6 gxh6 33 f6 h5 34 ♔e4 h4 35 ♔d5 h3

36 ♔c6

The entire episode – an equal position, a must win situation, half a

point lead in the final round, a hair-raising pawn race on opposite flanks – is strikingly reminiscent of the celebrated encounter Pillsbury – Gunsberg, from Hastings 1895. Indeed, history sometimes repeats itself.

36...♔e8

36...h2? succumbs to 37 ♔d7 h1=♕ 38 e7+.

37 ♗e5 a3 38 bxa3 ♗xa3 39 ♔xb5 h5 40 ♔c6 g4 41 ♔d5 h4 42 f7+ ♔f8 43 ♗f4 ♔g7 44 ♗d6 ♗xd6 45 ♔xd6 h2 46 ♔e7 h1=♕ 47 f8=♕+ ♔g6 48 ♕f6+ ♔h5 49 ♔f8 g3 50 e7 ♔g4 51 e8=♕ ♔h3 52 ♕8e6+ 1-0

A dry, quiet positional battle, may be transformed into a fierce tactical skirmish. It depends, to a large extent, on one's will and readiness to enter chaotic lines.

Andersson – Murey

Interzonal, Moscow 1982

1 ♘f3 d5 2 d4 c5 3 c4 e6 4 cxd5 exd5 5 g3 ♘c6 6 ♗g2 ♘f6 7 0-0 ♗e6 8 ♘c3 h6 9 ♗f4 ♖c8 10 ♖c1 a6 11 dxc5 ♗xc5 12 ♘e5 0-0 13 ♘xc6 ♖xc6 14 ♗e5 ♘g4 15 ♗d4 ♗xd4 16 ♕xd4 ♖c4 17 ♕a7

A critical juncture. 17...♕d7 18 ♖fd1 ♖fc8 keeps the fight going along positional channels – with White holding a slight edge because of the pressure on the isolated d5-pawn. Understandably, true to his style, Murey opts for a more dynamic solution.

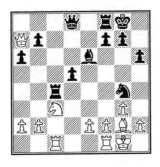

17...d4 18 ❨18❩ ♘e4 d3 19 exd3 ♖xc1 20 ♖xc1 ♕xd3 21 h3 ♘e5 22 ♘c3

22 ♕xb7?! ♘f3+ 23 ♗xf3 ♕xf3 is too risky.

22...b5 23 ♖d1 ♕c2 24 ♕d4

The position has opened up somewhat; still, it is solid, and continuations like 24...f6 or 24...♘c4 (25 b3 b4) would stay on a reasonable track. Now watch:

24...♕xb2! 25 ♖d2

25 ♕xe5 b4.

25...♕c1+ 26 ♖d1 ♕c2 27 ♗e4 ♗f5!!

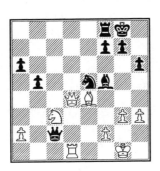

What a position! The board is on fire with three black pieces hanging. However, White cannot exploit this fact: 28 ♕xe5 ♗xe4; or 28 ♗xf5 ♘f3+.

Keeping his composure, Andersson selects the relatively best option:

28 ♗xc2! ♘f3+ 29 ♔f1 ♘xd4 30 ♗xf5 ♘xf5 31 ♘d5!

In this way White switches back to a sober position where his pawn minus is hardly significant.

31...♖a8 32 g4 ♘h4 33 ♖d3 f5 34 ♘e7+ ♔f7 35 ♘xf5 ♘xf5 36 gxf5 ♔f6 37 ♖d5 ♖a7 38 ♔g2 b4 39 ♖a5

The game is now balanced. **Black** later pressed too hard, and eventually **lost** on the 70th move.

Confusing the Issue

Miles – Korchnoi

Brussels 1986

1 d4 ♘f6 2 c4 g6 3 ♘c3 d5 4 ♘f3 ♗g7 5 e3 0-0 6 b4 b6 7 ♗b2 c5 8 bxc5 bxc5 9 dxc5 ♘a6 10 c6 ♘e4 11 ♘d4 ♖b8 12 ♕c1 ♕a5 13 f3 ♘ec5 14 ♘b3 ♕b4

White's opening has been a complete disaster. Disenchanted with lines such as 15 cxd5 ♘a4 16 ♔d2 ♘c7, White tries to flee with his king. Alas, it has no safe haven on the board.

15 ♔f2 ♘xb3 16 axb3 ♕xb3
17 ♖a2 d4 18 exd4 ♗xd4+ 19 ♔g3
♗e5+ 20 ♔h4

Incredulous glances from all readers, I suppose. But look at it this way: creating confusion by playing insane moves is the only practical fighting option here.

20...f6 21 ♕d2 ♘c7 22 ♗a1 ♘e6
23 ♘d5 g5+ 24 ♔h5 ♘g7+ 25 ♔h6

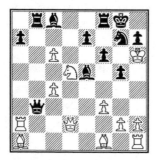

Black is intent on mating White's errant monarch. Meanwhile, White tries to form some counter-threats.

25...♘f5+ 26 ♔h5 ♕b1 27 ♗d3
♕xh1 28 ♗xe5 fxe5 29 h3 ♘g7+
30 ♔xg5 ♕h2 31 ♕e1 ♖f6 32 ♗xh7+
♔xh7 33 ♕h4+ ♔g8 34 ♘xf6+ exf6+
35 ♔g6

Give him one extra move, and White will blossom...

35...♗f5+ 36 ♔xf6 ♖f8+ 37 ♔e7
♕g1 38 ♕f2 ♕c1 39 ♔d6 ♕xc4
40 c7 ♖f6+ 0-1

Well, White was not rewarded for his outrageous play; but considering the alternatives, we would say that it was worth a try.

Gipslis – Smyslov

USSR championship, Tbilisi 1966

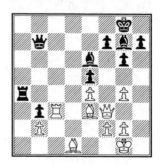

White to play

Black holds a considerable positional edge and White decides to take drastic measures.

32 ♖d3 h6 33 ♖d8+ ♔h7
34 ♗xh6!?

This shocking sacrifice dramatically changes the course of battle.

"The (observers) saw that after 34...♔xh6 35 ♕h3+ ♔g5 Black, a piece up, could save his king from perpetual check. To tell you the truth, I was sure that Smyslov would not capture the bishop, but... would look for some other continuations" – Tal. [27]

34...♕xe4?

Skipping the complications, but now the game peters out to a draw. Taking the king on a stroll is always a tough decision, but to gain victory here it was essential to choose this path: 34...♔xh6! (34...♗xh6?? 35 ♕f6 ♗g7 36 ♕h4+ ♗h6 37 g5) 35 ♕h3+ ♔g5 36 ♕h7 (36 g3 ♔f6; 36 ♕e3+ ♔f6 37 ♖e8 g5) ♕xe4! (36...♗f6?? 37 g3) 37 ♕xg7 ♖d4 with a winning endgame.

35 ♕xe4 ♖xe4 36 ♗xg7 ♔xg7
37 g5 ♖e1+ 38 ♔h2 f6 39 gxf6+
♔xf6 40 f3 ♗c4 41 ♔g3 ♔e6 42 ♖d2
½-½

Provocation

Inviting our rivals to punish our
'sins' by commencing an assault on
our position is a risky technique
which may easily backfire. Our first
example proves to be a success; the
second – a painful failure.

Salov – M. Gurevich

Reggio Emilia 1991

White to play

25 h3!

*"Trying to lure Black into various
attractive seeming combinations"* –
Salov. [28] Black is now offered two
inviting moves: 25...♘e3 and
25...♘xf2.

25...♘e3

Black yields to temptation.
25...♘e5 would have kept an edge
(25...♘xf2 is futile: 26 ♖xf2 ♗d4
27 ♘d1). Now the game is drawish.

26 fxe3 ♕xe3+ 27 ♔h2

Now 27...♕xc3 28 ♕xc3 ♗xc3
29 ♖c1 ♗e5 30 ♖xc4 f4 31 ♗f3
fxg3+ 32 ♔g2 is a dead draw. But
Black wants more:

27...f4? 28 ♖f3!

Not 28 gxf4 ♖xf4 29 ♘d5? ♖xf1!
30 ♘xe3 ♗e5 mate!

28...fxg3+ 29 ♖xg3! ♗e5

Black pins his hopes on this move;
29...♕xg3+ 30 ♔xg3 ♗e5+ 31 ♔g4
♖f4+ 32 ♔g5 is a brilliant, but losing
line.

30 ♖xh7+! 1-0

✓ Lasker – Steinitz

Hastings 1895

1 e4 e5 2 ♘f3 ♘c6 3 ♗b5 a6
4 ♗a4 d6 5 0-0 ♘e7 6 c3 ♗d7 7 d4
♘g6 8 ♖e1 ♗e7 9 ♘bd2 0-0 10 ♘f1
♕e8 11 ♗c2 ♔h8 12 ♘g3 ♗g4 13 d5

From now on, the ex-world
champion starts to reassemble his
troops awkwardly, along his first
rank.

**13...♘b8 14 h3 ♗c8 15 ♘f5 ♗d8
16 g4 ♘e7 17 ♘g3 ♘g8**

Whether Steinitz's play was
motivated by a peculiar sense of
humour (according to the German
Deutsche Schachzeitung); [29] a
profound plan of regrouping
(Reinfeld); or a deliberate desire to
provoke his adversary (our own
view) – the fact is that as a result of
his last moves, Black is severely
underdeveloped.

Steinitz practiced this sort of retrograde development on several occasions. For example, Tarrasch – Steinitz, Nuremberg 1896, went: 1 e4 e5 2 ♘f3 ♘c6 3 ♗b5 f6?! 4 0-0 ♘ge7 5 d4 ♘g6 6 a3 ♗e7 7 ♗c4 d6 8 h3 ♗d7 9 ♘c3 ♕c8 10 ♔h2 ♘d8!? 11 ♘d5 ♗f8 (1-0, 52).

Hereabouts, some White players would lose their temper and throw themselves at the insolent enemy. But that would only play into his hands. Emanuel Lasker knew better.

18 ♔g2 ♘d7 19 ♗e3 ♘b6 20 b3 ♗d7 21 c4 ♘c8

Somewhere around here Black crosses the boundary of what is reasonable. Shuffling pieces to and fro seldom brings positive results.

22 ♕d2 ♘ce7 23 c5 g6 24 ♕c3 f5 25 ♘xe5! dxe5 26 ♕xe5+ ♘f6 27 ♗d4

Correct. The hasty 27 g5? ♘exd5! is faulty.

27...fxg4 28 hxg4 ♗xg4 29 ♕g5 ♕d7 30 ♗xf6+ ♔g8 31 ♗d1 ♗h3+ 32 ♔g1 ♘xd5? 33 ♗xd8 ♘f4 34 ♗f6 ♕d2 35 ♖e2 ♘xe2+ 36 ♗xe2 ♕d7 37 ♖d1 ♕f7 38 ♗c4 ♗e6 39 e5 ♗xc4 40 ♘f5 1-0

Entering Incalculable Complications

'Devious chess' frequently involves entering unfathomable complications, the outcome of which is uncertain: a gamble unsuitable for the faint-hearted.

Minic – Tolush

Oberhausen 1961

1 e4 c5 2 ♘f3 d6 3 d4 cxd4 4 ♘xd4 ♘f6 5 ♘c3 a6 6 ♗c4 g6 7 f3 ♗g7 8 ♗e3 0-0 9 ♗b3 ♘c6 10 ♕d2 ♘a5 11 h4 ♘xb3 12 axb3 h5 13 ♗h6 ♗d7 14 g4 hxg4 15 h5 e5 16 ♗g5?! exd4 17 ♘d5

A very sharp position has arisen. Black's queenside attack is seriously delayed so White decided to sacrifice a piece to pursue his own attack.

17...♖e8?

17...gxf3! is stronger, e.g. 18 h6 f2+ 19 ♕xf2 ♘xe4 20 hxg7 ♕xg5 21 ♕h2 ♗h3! 22 gxf8=♕+ ♖xf8 with a decisive advantage for Black.

18 h6

Black appears on the verge of collapse: 18...♗h8 19 h7+ ♔g7 (19...♔f8? 20 ♗h6+ ♗g7 21 h8=♕+) 20 ♗h6+ ♔xh7 21 ♗g5+ ♔g8 22 ♖xh8+ is a sample of the horrendous fate awaiting him.

18...gxf3

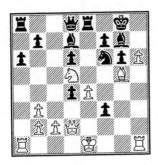

19 hxg7

19 0-0-0 ♘xe4 20 ♗xd8 ♘xd2 21 ♘f6+ ♗xf6 22 ♗xf6 loses to 22...♘xb3+ 23 cxb3 ♖ac8+ 24 ♔b1 ♔h7.

19...♘xe4 20 ♗e7?

A beautiful but erroneous move. From all the possible lines at his disposal, it was difficult to hit on the correct path. 20 ♖h8+! ♔xg7 21 ♗xd8 ♘xd2+ 22 ♖xe8 ♗xe8 23 ♗f6+ ♔h6 24 ♔xd2 g5 25 ♘e7 ♔h5 26 ♖g1 is winning for White.

20...f2+! 21 ♕xf2 ♖xe7 22 ♖h8+

Better is 22 ♕h4 ♘f6+ 23 ♔f1 ♘h5 24 ♘xe7+ ♔xg7 25 ♕xd4+ f6 with an unclear position.

22...♔xg7 23 ♕xd4+ ♘f6+ 24 ♔d2 ♖e4 25 ♖h7+ ♔xh7 26 ♘xf6+ ♔g7 27 ♘xe4+ f6 28 ♖e1 ♕a5+ 29 b4 ♕e5

White has been on the offensive throughout the whole game but his rewards are dismal. Chess may be cruel at times.

30 ♕xd6 ♕xd6 31 ♘xd6 ♗c6 32 ♘xb7 ♗xb7 33 ♖e7+ ♔h6 34 ♖xb7 g5 35 c4 g4 36 ♔e3 ♔g5 (**0-1**, 56 moves)

Opportunism

The books tell us that chess is not a random game and that things do have a reason. Strong plans develop from sound opening systems; tactics lean on the shoulders of strategy.

Nevertheless there are exceptions where something springs out of nowhere. When such things happen we must ensure that we are there to grab the chance.

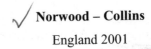

Norwood – Collins

England 2001

1 g3 d5 2 ♗g2 c6 3 ♘f3 ♗g4 4 b3 ♘d7 5 ♗b2 ♘gf6 6 0-0 e6 7 d3 ♗d6 8 ♘bd2 0-0 9 h3 ♗h5 10 e4 dxe4 11 dxe4 ♗e5 12 c3 ♗c7 13 ♕e2 ♘e5 14 g4 ♘xf3+ 15 ♗xf3 ♗g6

So far, the game has been a mundane affair. Now White spots an idea:

16 ♗a3 ♖e8

16...♗d6? 17 ♗xd6 ♕xd6 18 e5.

17 ♖ad1

The black queen will come under fire from a white rook, and White plans to plant a piece on d6 (via ♘c4).

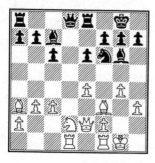

17...♘d5!!

Do me a favour, don't try to find the positional justification of why this move works. It just does. I don't believe Black had entertained any evil thoughts earlier on: his 16...♖e8 was compulsory, and contained no threat; it is only 17 ♖ad1!?, robbing White's queen of the flight square d1, which makes the knight leap viable.

18 ♘c4

18 exd5? exd5 is catastrophic, and the threats 18...♘xc3 and ♘f4 are imminent. White gives up material.

18...♘xc3 19 ♕e3 ♘xd1 20 ♖xd1 ♕h4 21 ♔g2 ♖ed8

Black has a decisive advantage – which he later spoilt and the game was **drawn** on the 63rd move.

Nezhmetdinov – Aronin

USSR 1953

1 e4 c5 2 ♘f3 d6 3 g3 ♘c6 4 ♗g2 ♗g4 5 h3 ♗h5 6 d3 e6 7 ♘c3 ♗e7 8 0-0 ♗f6

6...♘f6 is more common but the text move is acceptable.

9 ♘e2 ♗xf3

Black doesn't fancy an eventual g3-g4-g5 and exchanges his ♗h5 straight away.

10 ♗xf3 ♘ge7 11 ♗g2 d5 12 exd5?!

12 f4 or 12 c3 is superior.

12...♘xd5 13 ♘f4 ♘xf4 14 ♗xf4

14 ♗xc6+ bxc6 15 ♗xf4 ♗xb2 doesn't promise much.

14...♕d7 15 c3

This weakens d3. Perhaps 15 ♖ab1 with the plan a3 and b4, gives better chances.

15...0-0

White possesses the bishop pair, but Black's formation is rock solid. The late Rashid Nezhmetdinov was a brilliant tactician, endowed with a creative and fertile imagination. It is interesting to witness his approach to a type of colourless position which is not to his taste.

16 ♕a4 ♖ac8

Correct. There is no sense entering variations like 16...♕xd3 17 ♖ad1 ♕e2 18 ♖d2 ♕h5 19 ♖d7, when the white bishop pair springs to life.

17 ♖ad1 ♖fd8

Black provides firm protection against White's intended opening of the position with d3-d4.

18 ♖fe1 b6?!

This natural idea, while not really an error, grants White some chances.

19 ♕a6!

Prophylaxis: Black would like to transfer his knight to d5, but this is now prevented: if 19...♘e7? then 20 ♗b7! annexes the exchange. Another Black plan, 19...e5, is now unattractive because of 20 ♗xc6 ♖xc6 21 ♗xe5 ♕xh3 22 ♕b7.

19...g5?

An ugly, totally unnecessary weakening; instead, he should play 19...♘b8 20 ♕b7 ♘c6 with an adequate position. It is instructive to see how even strong players frequently make bad moves once their plans are foiled.

20 ♗c1 ♘a5

20...♘e7 21 f4! is to White's advantage. But Black's choice is strange; perhaps he wanted to keep the ♕a6 boxed in, but...

21 d4!

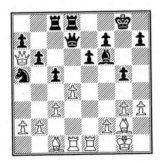

21...cxd4

Or 21...c4 22 d5! and the power of the bishops will shortly manifest itself.

22 ♕e2

The white queen is going east: a dramatic movement from a6, where it harassed Black's queenside, to h5,

targeting the king. One error from the enemy (19...g5?) and a manoeuvre that was senseless a move ago becomes powerful. This is opportunism at its best.

22...h6?!

22...d3 23 ♕f3 is bad; and 22...♕e7 23 ♕h5 dxc3 24 ♗e4 cxb2 25 ♗xg5! is one nasty line to avoid. But 22...♕e7! 23 ♕h5 dxc3 24 ♗e4 ♔f8! holds; for instance, 25 ♕xh7 ♖xd1 26 ♖xd1 ♖d8.

23 ♕h5 ♔g7 24 h4 ♕e7 25 cxd4 ♘c4 26 b3 ♘d6 27 d5!

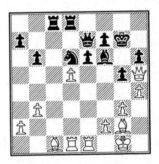

We've been on the queenside, we've been on the kingside, and now the decisive thrust occurs in the centre.

27...e5? 28 f4 gxf4 29 ♗xf4 ♖h8 30 ♖xe5 ♕d7

30...♗xe5 31 ♕xe5+.

31 ♖e2 ♖h7?

A crude error which shortens Black's agony. Admittedly, 31...♕f5 32 ♕xf5 ♘xf5 33 ♗e4 is scarcely an improvement.

32 ♗xd6 1-0

32...♕xd6 33 ♕g4+ with 34 ♕xc8.

Striving for Imbalance

One way to enliven an equal position is to create a state of positional or material imbalance.

Diaz – Palatnik

Caracas 1976

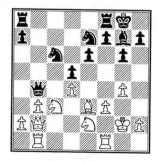

Black to play

20...♘xd4! 21 a3 ♘xe2

There is no way back: 21...♕b6? 22 ♘a4 ♕xb3 23 ♗xd4 favours White.

22 axb4 ♘xc3 23 ♗h6!? ♗xh6 24 ♕xc3 ♖fc8 25 ♕f6 ♖c7

For his queen Black has two knights and a pawn; theoretically, insufficient remuneration. However, his solid formation renders him immune from the risk of losing; and he might achieve something with his passed d-pawn.

26 b5 ♖ac8 27 ♕d4 ♗g7 28 ♕g1 ♗c3 29 b6 axb6 30 ♕xb6 d4 31 ♔h1 ♘d5 32 ♕d6 d3 33 ♖fd1 ♗b4 34 ♕a6 d2

We feel that with each turn the game swings in Black's direction.

35 ♖xd2 ♗xd2 36 h4 ♘f4 37 b4 ♗xb4! 0-1

The follow up will be 38 ♖xb4 ♖c1+ 39 ♔h2 ♖8c2+ 40 ♔g3 e5 41 ♖xf4 ♖g1+ 42 ♔h3 exf4.

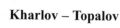

Kharlov – Topalov

World championship,
Tripoli 2004

1 e4 e5 2 ♗c4 ♘f6 3 d3 c6 4 ♘f3 ♗e7 5 0-0 d6 6 a4 0-0 7 ♖e1 ♘bd7 8 ♘c3 ♘c5 9 d4 exd4 10 ♘xd4 a5 11 ♗f4 ♘g4 12 ♗e2 ♘f6 13 ♗f3 ♖e8 14 ♕d2 g6 15 h3 ♘fd7 16 ♖ad1 ♗f8 17 g4 ♕b6 18 ♗g2 ♘e5 19 b3 ♕b4 20 ♘de2

White has a very solid and promising formation: the weakness of Black's d-pawn gives White a slight but nagging pull. Topalov, who needed only a draw to qualify for the next stage, goes for a drastic disturbance of the equilibrium.

20...f6 21 ♗e3 h5 22 f4 ♘xg4! 23 hxg4 ♗xg4 24 ♕c1 f5 25 ♖d4 ♕b6 26 ♕d2 ♕c7 27 ♗f2 ♖e6 28 ♖c4 ♖ae8 29 ♘d4 ♖xe4! 30 ♘xe4 ♘xe4 31 ♗xe4 fxe4

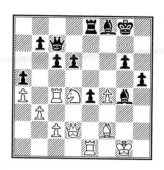

White is a rook ahead, but it is not evident how he is going to break the formidable black pawn-chain.

32 ♖c3 d5 33 ♖g3 ♗d6 34 ♗e3 ♕d7 35 c3 ♖f8 36 ♖f1 b6 37 ♖f2 c5 38 ♘b5 ♗b8 39 ♖fg2 g5 40 ♖f2

"White has two problems: his knight is out of play, and the light squares around his king are weak" – Kavalek. [30]

40...♔g7 41 ♕c1 ♔g6 42 ♕f1 ♖f5 43 ♖gg2 ♕f7 44 fxg5 ♗f3 45 ♖h2 ♗xh2+ 46 ♖xh2 ♖f4!! 47 ♗xf4 ♕xf4

Now 48 ♕h3 may be objectively best but Black can force an immediate draw with 48...♕c1+. Due to the match situation, White avoids this line, and later on stumbles and loses.

48 ♖g2 h4 49 ♕e1 e3 50 ♖h2 ♕xg5+ 51 ♔f1 h3 52 ♕b1+? ♗e4 53 ♕b2 ♗d3+ 0-1

Desperados

When a player feels that the fight is lost, he may go out peacefully and resign himself to his fate. Alternatively, he might – and should – make a last vehement attempt to change the result.

The best desperate attacks are those which appear to hold no chances. They are so ridiculous that our opponent does not take them seriously.

Fazekas – N. Littlewood

British championship 1963

1 ♘f3 g6 2 c4 ♗g7 3 ♘c3 d6 4 d4 ♗g4 5 e3 e5 6 ♗e2 ♘c6 7 0-0 ♘ge7 8 d5 ♘b8 9 h3 ♗d7 10 b4 0-0 11 ♖b1 f5 12 c5 ♗f6 13 ♘d2 g5 14 e4 ♗e8 **15** ♘c4 a6 16 cxd6 cxd6 17 ♗e3 b5 18 ♘a5 ♔h8 19 f3 ♖g8 20 ♖c1 f4 21 ♗f2 ♘g6 22 a4

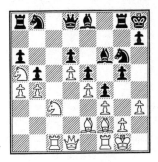

The best we can do to describe Black's play, so far, is to hold our tongue. Around here he must have felt that if things proceeded normally, say 22...bxa4 23 ♘xa4 ♘d7 24 ♘c6, he would be wiped out. Hence he throws all caution to the wind and rushes forward.

22...♗d7 23 axb5 ♕f8?! 24 b6 ♕h6 25 b7 ♗xh3 26 bxa8=♕ ♗xg2 27 ♔xg2 g4 28 ♖h1 gxf3+

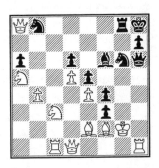

White has amassed quite a fortune over the last few moves. He is now a queen, rook and bishop ahead (!). All he need do is avoid being mated. The simple 29 ♗xf3 suffices, as the discovered, double-check (29...♘h4++) is nothing (30 ♔f1).

29 ♔xf3?? ♘h4+ 30 ♔xh4 ♗xh4

Amazingly, White is helpless.

31 ♖xh4 ♕xh4 32 ♕g1 ♕h3+ 0-1

Timman – Kasparov

Bugojno 1982

1 d4 ♘f6 2 c4 g6 3 ♘c3 ♗g7 4 e4 d6 5 f3 0-0 6 ♗e3 ♘c6 7 ♘ge2 a6 8 ♕d2 ♖b8 9 h4 b5 10 h5 e5 11 d5 ♘a5 12 ♘g3 bxc4 13 0-0-0 ♘d7 14 hxg6 fxg6 15 ♘b1 ♖b5?

15...♘b7 16 ♗xc4 ♘bc5 is correct.

16 b4!

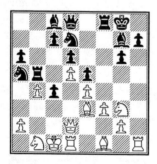

This thrust refutes Black's 15th move. 16...♘b7 17 ♗xc4 is hopeless.

16...cxb3 e.p. 17 ♗xb5 c5

"It is absurd to say that Black is on the verge of defeat – he has already crossed this verge!" – Kasparov. [31] He suggests 18 ♗e2 as the simplest winning line.

18 dxc6 e.p.?! axb5 19 ♕d5+?

19 cxd7 ♘c4 20 dxc8=♕ ♕xc8 21 ♕d5+ ♖f7 is no longer so simple but, instead of 21 ♕d5, 21 axb3! ♘xd2+ 22 ♔xd2 would have won (Kasparov).

19...♖f7 20 axb3 ♘f8 21 ♕xd6 ♕e8 22 ♕d8 ♕xc6+ 23 ♔b2 ♕a8! 24 ♖c1 ♘c4+ 25 bxc4 ♖d7! 26 ♕e8 bxc4 27 ♘c3 ♕c6!

How things have changed! Black now wins the white queen by dint of the threats ...♖d2+ and ...♖b7+.

28 ♔c2 ♖d2+ ½-½

Both protagonists have had enough excitement for the day. Objectively, though, after 29 ♔xd2 ♕xe8 30 ♘d5, White is still better.

Karolyi – Hodgson

Icklicki Masters 1989

1 d4 d6 2 ♘f3 ♗g4 3 ♘bd2 ♘f6 4 c4 ♘bd7 5 h3 ♗h5 6 g4 ♗g6 7 ♗g2 e5 8 ♘h4 c6 9 ♘xg6 hxg6 10 e3 d5 11 0-0 e4 12 cxd5 cxd5 13 f3 ♗b4 14 g5 ♘h7 15 h4

15...♘xg5

"We looked at each other (in disbelief) and laughed. We both knew

that this cannot be correct; but if Black is already lost, perhaps this is the best practical chance." – Karolyi. [32]

16 hxg5 ♕xg5 17 ♖f2 0-0-0 18 fxe4 ♖h5

Now 19 ♘f3 ♕g3 20 e5 ♖dh8 21 ♔f1 leaves Black with nothing to show for his material deficit.

However, White is oblivious of the dangers inherent in the position.

19 ♕b3? ♖dh8 20 ♔f1 ♗xd2 21 ♖xd2? ♖h1+ 22 ♗xh1 ♖xh1+ 23 ♔e2 ♘c5!! 24 dxc5 dxe4

The knight sacrifice has blocked the c-file, thus preventing the saving 25 ♕c4+. Now the white king is doomed.

25 ♖d8+ ♕xd8 0-1

Chapter Nine:

Confronting 'Devious Chess'

Let us investigate 'devious chess' from the other side of the board; that is, from the viewpoint of a player who plays a correct, solid, well-founded game, but encounters an opponent who employs a 'different' kind of chess. How ought one to oppose unconventional conduct?

Basically, there are four ways to handle this task. One way is *prevention*: to avoid all shades of tricky positions, before they loom on the board. A second alternative is to let tricky situations occur, but *to ignore* them, staying firmly on the main road. A third practice is *simplification*: to liquidate material as soon as 'devious chess' occurs, directing the play towards 'normal' sort of play. Finally, there is the method of seeking a clear *refutation*: to allow unconventional positions to emerge, aiming to exploit their deficiencies.

Preventing

Botvinnik – T. Petrosian

World championship match,
Moscow 1963

1 d4 d5 2 c4 dxc4 3 ♘f3 ♘f6 4 e3 e6 5 ♗xc4 c5 6 0-0 a6 7 a4 ♘c6

8 ♕e2 ♗e7 9 dxc5 ♗xc5 10 e4 ♘g4 11 e5

At the time, this was a stunning novelty. White sacrifices his e-pawn for some initiative.

11...♘d4 12 ♘xd4 ♕xd4 13 ♘a3 ♗xa3

The immediate 13...♘xe5 is uninviting: White can choose between the solid 14 ♗e3 ♕d6 15 ♖fd1 and Tal's more radical suggestion 14 b4!? ♘xc4 15 ♘xc4 ♕xa1 16 bxc5.

14 ♖xa3 ♘xe5 15 b3

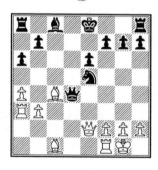

A critical position from which some fascinating variations were unearthed in the press room.

15...♘xc4 16 bxc4 0-0 17 ♖g3 f6 18 ♗h6 ♖f7 19 ♖d1 ♕b6 20 ♕b2! ♕c7 21 ♖xg7+! ♖xg7 22 ♕xf6 and wins – D.Bronstein – see diagram.

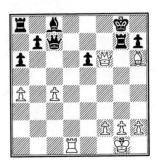

(variation)

Or: 15...♘g6 16 ♗b2 ♕d6 17 ♖d1 ♕c5 18 ♗xg7 ♕xa3 19 ♗b5+!! ♔e7 (19...axb5 20 ♕xb5+ ♔e7 21 ♕g5+, mating) 20 ♕f3! f5 21 ♕c3! with mate threats on c7 and f6 – Smyslov. [33]

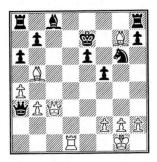

(variation)

And in the game? Well, Petrosian had a well-developed sense of danger and he would have nothing of such suicidal lines!

15...♕c5 16 ♖a2?! ♘xc4 17 bxc4 ♗d7 18 ♗a3 ♕f5! 19 ♖d2 ♗c6 20 ♖e1 h5 21 ♕e3 f6!

White threatened 22 ♖d5! ♗xd5 23 ♕c5 ♕f6 24 cxd5 with a dominating position. The text move returns the pawn to kill White's attack.

22 ♕xe6+ ♕xe6 23 ♖xe6+ ♔f7 24 ♖e7+ ♔g6

Having deftly extricated himself from the complications by refusing to enter them, Black now holds a minute positional edge. The game was **drawn** on the 55th move.

Ignoring

Karpov – Spassky

Candidates match, Leningrad 1974

1 d4 ♘f6 2 c4 g6 3 ♘c3 ♗g7 4 e4 d6 5 ♘f3 0-0 6 ♗e2 c5 7 0-0 ♗g4 8 d5 ♘bd7 9 ♗g5 a6 10 a4 ♕c7 11 ♕d2 ♖ae8 12 h3 ♗xf3 13 ♗xf3 e6 14 b3 ♔h8 15 ♗e3 ♘g8 16 ♗e2 e5 17 g4 ♕d8 18 ♔g2 ♕h4?! 19 f3

19 ♗g5 is met by 19...♗h6.

19...♗h6? 20 g5 ♗g7 21 ♗f2 ♕f4 22 ♗e3 ♕h4

Black had deliberately stuck his queen in an awkward position. Most players, as White, would seek a way to take advantage of the vulnerable black queen. But Karpov is not to be diverted: he finds a clear plan, connected with fixing Black's queenside pawns and breaking through on the b-file, which leads to his advantage. He now swaps queens to increase the impact of this plan.

23 ♕e1! ♕xe1 24 ♖fxe1 h6 25 h4 hxg5 26 hxg5 ♘e7 27 a5 f6 28 ♖eb1! fxg5 29 b4

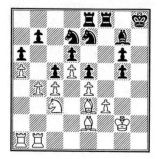

29...♘f5!

A bold attempt to get back into the game. After 30 exf5 e4! 31 ♗d2 exf3+ 32 ♗xf3 gxf5 there is some life left in Black's camp. Whether the piece sacrifice is correct or not, remains behind the scenes, as White ignores the bait without blinking.

30 ♗xg5! ♘d4

30...♗h6 31 exf5 ♗xg5 32 ♘e4 is no better.

31 bxc5 ♘xc5 32 ♖b6! ♗f6 33 ♖h1+ ♔g7

Or 33...♔g8 34 ♖xd6! ♗xg5 35 ♖xg6+.

34 ♗h6+ ♔g8 35 ♗xf8 ♖xf8 36 ♖xd6 (1-0, 55).

Simplifying

Employing an exchanging policy or some other method of simplifying the position, narrows the possibilities of our adversaries to indulge in unconventional chess.

Ree – Kupreichik

Hastings 1981

1 d4 d5 2 c4 c6 3 ♘c3 ♘f6 4 e3 e6 5 ♘f3 ♘bd7 6 ♕c2 ♗d6 7 b3 0-0 8 ♗b2 a6 9 ♗e2 dxc4 10 bxc4 c5 11 0-0 cxd4 12 exd4 b6 13 a4 ♗b7 14 ♗a3 ♗xa3 15 ♖xa3 ♖c8 16 ♘d2 ♕e7 17 ♕b2 ♕d6

Black is slightly better, owing to White's fragile pawn-centre. In response, White embarks on an interesting plan:

18 ♘d1 a5 19 c5?! ♕c6 20 ♘e3 bxc5 21 ♗f3 ♘d5 22 dxc5

The c-pawn is doomed, but White hopes to obtain counter-chances, as 22...♘xc5? 23 ♗xd5 exd5 24 ♘f5! is strong. On other lines, ♖a3 will be transferred to the king's flank, to target g7 and h7

Black reacts by simplifying the position.

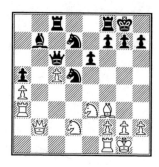

22...♕a6! 23 ♗xd5 ♗xd5 24 ♘xd5 exd5 25 ♖g3 g6 26 ♕d4

It appears as if White has made some progress: d5 is hanging and the dark squares near the black king are weakened.

26...♘xc5! 27 ♕xd5 ♖fd8 28 ♕g5 ♘e6

29 ♕e3

On 29 ♕h6, 29...♖c2 is strong (30 ♘e4?? ♕xf1+, mating).

29...♘d4

In spite of the simple nature of the position, Black maintains a pronounced initiative. No less important: his position is rock solid, with no 'tricks' for White.

30 ♖h3 ♘e2+ 31 ♔h1 ♖xd2!

Another simplifying operation.

32 ♕xd2 ♘f4 33 ♖c1 ♘xh3 34 gxh3 ♖xc1+ 35 ♕xc1 ♕d3

The predicament of the white king is pathetic, his pawns are shattered. Black is winning.

36 ♕c8+ ♔g7 37 ♔g2 ♕e4+ 38 ♔g3 h5! 39 ♕c3+ ♔g8 40 f4 h4+ 0-1

Ciric – Kelecevic

Sarajevo 1968

1 e4 c5 2 ♘f3 e6 3 d4 cxd4 4 ♘xd4 ♘f6 5 ♘c3 ♗b4 6 e5 ♘e4?! 7 ♕g4 ♕a5 8 ♕xe4 ♗xc3+ 9 bxc3 ♕xc3+ 10 ♔d1 ♕xa1 11 ♘b5 d5 12 exd6 e.p. ♘a6 13 d7+ ♗xd7 14 ♘d6+ ♔e7 15 ♗xa6 ♗c6 16 ♘f5+ ♔e8

An ultra-sharp opening variation has given rise to a turbulent situation. It is instructive to observe how White now tames the lion, liquidating pieces to reach a winning endgame, almost by force.

17 ♕b4! ♖d8+

17...exf5? 18 ♖e1+ ♗e4 19 ♗b5+ ♔d8 20 ♕d6+ ♔c8 21 ♗d7+ with a quick mate.

18 ♘d6+ ♔e7 19 ♔e2!! ♕e5+

White threatened 20 ♗g5+, winning the queen. 19...♕xa2 falls short against 20 ♘c8++ ♔f6 (20...♔d7 21 ♕d6+ ♔xc8 22 ♕xc6+) 21 ♕f4+.

20 ♘e4+ ♔e8 21 ♗xb7! ♗xb7 22 ♕xb7 f5 23 ♗g5 ♕xe4+ 24 ♕xe4 fxe4 25 ♗xd8 ♔xd8 26 ♖b1

26...♔c7 27 ♖b4 ♔d6 28 ♖b7! ♖c8 29 ♔d2 ♖f8 30 ♔e3 ♖c8 31 ♖xa7 (1-0, 63 moves)

Refuting

If the opponent's play is basically unsound, then one must be ready to fight bravely to refute his play. The refutation may not be easy and could entail significant risks: extreme measures might be required to repulse a vehement onslaught.

Tal – Keres

Candidates tournament, Bled 1959

White to play

Instead of the natural 17 0-0, Tal opted for a reckless sacrificial sequence:

17 ♘b6?! ♗g4 18 ♕c2 ♘xd3+ 19 ♕xd3 ♖a6 20 0-0 ♖xb6 21 ♗d6?!

This was White's idea. While Black takes time to capture material, White opens files and trains his guns against the enemy king.

21...♕xd6 22 e5 ♕e7!

A simple yet strong riposte. 23 exf6? now fails to 23...♕e3+, thus Black seizes a necessary tempo to organize his defences.

23 ♖ae1 ♘d7 24 e6 fxe6 25 c5 ♘xc5 26 ♕g6+ ♔d8 27 b4

All this looks like absolute rubbish but during this period Tal used to score many points against top players from similarly random positions.

27...axb4 28 ♕xg4 cxd5 29 ♕g3 ♘d7 30 axb4 ♖f8 (0-1, 40 moves)

Arkell – A. Ledger

4NCL 2001

White to play

21 ♔f2!

White holds a positional edge, based mainly on his better pawn structure. He is not afraid of defending e3 with his monarch. To exploit the king's sortie, Black makes material concessions which White welcomes.

21...♘d7 22 ♖c2 ♘f6 23 e4! ♗xe4

Black takes his chance to force his opponent's king into the open.

24 fxe4 ♗e3+?!

24...♘g4+ 25 ♔g1 ♗e3+ 26 ♔h1 ♘f2+ 27 ♖xf2 ♗xf2 28 ♗h3 is unpromising for Black.

25 ♔xe3 ♘g4+ 26 ♔f3 ♖d3+ 27 ♔xg4

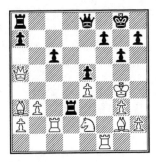

White acts bravely and is not scared of ghosts. His king is not happy in the open air, but Black lacks sufficient material to end the job.

27...♕e6+ 28 ♔h4 h5

Or 28...g5+ 29 ♔h5 ♕g6+ 30 ♔g4 h5+ 31 ♔h3 g4+ 32 ♔h4 f6 33 ♖f5 and Black's attack runs out of steam (Palliser).

29 h3! g5+ 30 ♔xh5 g4 31 ♖f5 ♔h7 32 ♔h4 ♖h8 33 ♖h5+ ♔g7 34 hxg4 1-0

Hazai – Karsa

Hungarian championship,
Budapest 1976

1 e4 e5 2 ♘f3 ♘c6 3 ♗b5 ♘f6 4 ♗xc6 dxc6 5 d3 ♗d6 6 ♘bd2 c5 7 ♘c4 ♕e7 8 ♗g5 h6 9 ♗h4 ♗g4 10 h3 ♗h5 11 ♘e3 ♗g6 12 g4 0-0-0 13 ♘d2 h5 14 ♘f5 ♗xf5 15 gxf5 ♕d7 16 ♘c4 ♖dg8 17 ♕d2 ♘h7 18 ♕c3 f6 19 ♖g1

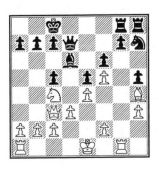

Black's position is restricted and White is slowly increasing his space advantage. To gain counterplay, Black embarks upon a sharp, imaginative line:

19...g5?! 20 fxg6 e.p. ♕xh3 21 g7

21 ♘xd6+ cxd6 22 g7 ♕xh4 is not so clear.

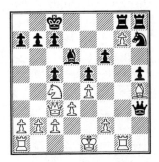

Now White invites 21...♖xg7 22 ♖xg7 ♕h1+ 23 ♔e2 ♕xa1 24 ♘xd6+ cxd6 25 ♕a5 mating.

21...♗f8?!

An astonishing concept.

22 gxh8=♕

22 gxf8=♕+? ♖xf8 and Black regains his piece, since the ♗h4 has no flight squares (23 ♗g3 h4).

22...♖xg1+ 23 ♔d2 ♖xa1

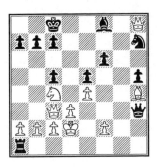

We have to admire Black for his grandiose concept, allowing

(actually, forcing!) White to promote to a second queen in return for dangerous counter-threats. However, respecting our opponent's schemes should not deter us from refuting them...

24 ♕b3

Envisaging 24...♕f1, White vacates c3 for his king. In addition, the queen move assists him in rounding off his own attack.

24...♕xh4 25 ♘d6+ cxd6 26 ♕e6+ ♔d8 27 ♕xd6+ ♔c8 28 ♕xc5+ ♔b8 29 ♕d6+ ♔c8 30 ♕g8?!

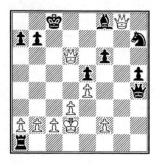

30...♕g4

A crude error, but 30...♕xf2+ 31 ♔c3 ♕d4+ 32 ♕xd4 exd4+ 33 ♔xd4 only prolongs Black's agony.

31 ♕c4 mate.

*   *   *   *

Castro – Y. Geller

Interzonal, Biel 1976

White to play

White is worse in this position, and the continuations 21 ♘e3 ♘a5 or 21 ♘d2 ♕e5 do not promise a positive result. Therefore, he tries to change course:

21 ♖d1

Question: Black can now choose between several paths. He may *ignore* the bait by, say, 21...♗f8, e.g. 22 ♘e3 (22 ♗xf8 bxc4 23 ♗xc4 ♘a5; or 22 ♘d6 ♗xd6 23 ♖xd5 ♗h2+) ♗xc5; he may *simplify* with 21...♘f4 22 ♖xd8+ ♘xd8; or he can attempt to *refute* White's play, by 21...bxc4 22 ♗xc4 ♘a5. What would you play?

Part Three:

Illustrative Games

This part of the book illuminates, with the aid of 15 complete games, the concept of 'devious chess'. The samples I have chosen are varied. Some are wild and extraordinary to such an extent that their distinction is evident (for example, Gaprindashvili – Ujtelky). In several of these games, naked kings walk in mid-board, with all sorts of bizarre material imbalances.

Other samples are more conventional, almost 'normal', exemplifying vividly one or several aspects of 'devious chess' (e.g. Bellini – Pelletier). There are games which concentrate on the opening stage (Zaitseva – Stjazhkina), while others offer a spectacular middle-game (Korchnoi – Morozevich), or even a fascinating endgame (Tate – Ashley). Most games feature tactical fantasies but some are positionally profound (like Keres – T. Petrosian). I have tried to pick games which are analytically sound, but then again, some (like Marshall – Atkins) are essentially bluffs.

Game 1

D. Bronstein – Gulko

Moscow championship 1968

1	e4	e6
2	d4	d5
3	♘d2	c5
4	exd5	exd5
5	♗b5+	♘c6
6	♘e2	

6 ♘gf3 is the usual line.

6	...	♛b6
7	a4	♘f6
8	0-0	♗g4
9	h3	♗h5
10	c3	cxd4?

Prematurely opening up the position.

| 11 | g4! | ♗g6 |

11...dxc3 is met advantageously by 12 ♘xc3 ♗g6 13 g5 followed by 14 ♘xd5.

| 12 | ♘xd4 | |

| 12 | ... | 0-0-0?! |

A dubious move, but Black's position is already precarious, as he has to provide against the threat of 13 a5 ♕c7 14 a6. Soviet sources suggested 12...a6 13 ♗xc6+ bxc6 14 ♖e1+ ♗e7 15 ♕e2 0-0 (?) and if 16 ♕xe7?? ♖fe8. However, 16 a5! wins outright.

13	a5	♕c7
14	a6	♘xd4
15	axb7+	♔b8

15...♕xb7? 16 ♗a6.

| 16 | cxd4 | |

By playing simple and natural moves, White has obtained a dream position.

| 16 | ... | ♗c2 |

Forced; if the white queen is permitted to reach a4, Black may as well throw in the towel.

| 17 | ♕e2 | |

There can be no doubt that Black is fighting a lost cause. White has a simple winning plan: ♘f3-e5-c6+.

| 17 | ... | h5! |

The best practical chance. Black creates the *illusion* of a serious counter-attack and diverts White's attention towards defending his own king.

| 18 | g5? | |

White falls into a psychological trap. Rather than attempt to close lines on the king-flank, he should pursue his basic plan. This would have proven decisive within several moves: 18 ♘f3!, and now: 18...♘xg4 (18...♗d6 19 g5 ♘h7 20 ♗e3) 19 hxg4 hxg4 20 ♘e5 ♗e4 21 ♕xe4! dxe4 22 ♘c6+, winning; or 18...hxg4 19 ♘e5 ♖xh3 20 ♘c6+ ♕xc6 21 ♗xc6 ♗e4 22 f3 gxf3 23 ♗f4+ ♗d6 24 ♗xd6+ ♖xd6 25 ♕a6.

If, after 18...hxg4 19 ♘e5, Black tries to improve with the cunning 19...♖d6 20 ♗f4 ♖xh3, he succumbs to 21 ♖fc1! ♗e4 22 ♕xe4 ♘xe4 23 ♖xc7 ♔xc7 24 ♖xa7 when he is helpless against 25 b8=♕++ ♔xb8 26 ♘c6+ ♔c8 27 ♗a6 mate (analysis by Gulko). [34]

18	...	♘g4
19	f4	f6
20	hxg4?	

The battle is heated and making the right moves necessitates precise calculation. Here 20 ♖a6!, intending 21 ♖c6, still assures White the upper hand after either 20...♖d6 21 hxg4 hxg4 22 ♕xg4 or 20...♗f5 21 ♖c6 ♕xb7 22 ♘b3 ♗b4 23 ♘c5.

20	...	hxg4
21	♗a4	♗f5
22	♕a6	♗c5!
23	dxc5	♕xc5+
24	♔g2	♕e3

The initiative has passed to Black. He is threatening 25...♖h2+!

26 ♔xh2 ♕h3+ 27 ♔g1 ♕g3+ 28 ♔h1 ♖h8 mate.

25	♖a3	♗e4+
26	♘xe4	♕xe4+
27	♔g3	♖h3+

Careful! The tempting 27...f5 permits 28 ♕xa7+! ♔xa7 29 ♗c2+.

| 28 | ♔xg4 | ♕g2+ |
| 29 | ♔f5 | fxg5! |

Black can already force a draw (29...♕e4+ 30 ♔g4 ♕g2+) but he strives for more.

White is two bishops ahead but the plight of his king leaves much to be desired. Bronstein plays a natural move – exchanging rooks in the hope of decreasing the enemy's force. However, Black's remaining queen and rook are powerful enough to deliver the *coup de grace*.

30 ♖xh3?

There is an amazing saving resource: 30 ♗e8!!, cutting off the ♖d8 from f8 and at the same time uniting White's heavy pieces along the a-file, threatening 31 ♕xa7+ followed by mate. Had White played 30 ♗e8!! Black would have had to take a draw by 30...♕e4+ 31 ♔g4 ♕g2+.

| 30 | ... | ♖f8+ |
| 31 | ♔g6 | |

31 ♔e6 ♕e4+ 32 ♔d6 ♖f6+ followed by 33...♖xa6.

But now the white king is led to a final march from where there is no return.

31	...	gxf4+
32	♔h7	♕xh3+
33	♔xg7	♕h8+
34	♔g6	♖g8+
35	♔f5	♕h7+!
36	♔e5	

Or 36 ♔xf4 ♕e4 mate.

36	...	♕e4+
37	♔d6	♖g6+
38	♔c5	♖xa6
39	♗xf4+	♔xb7
40	♗b5	♖a5

0-1

Game 2

Marshall – Atkins

USA – Great Britain cable match
1903

1	d4	d5
2	c4	c6
3	♘c3	♘f6
4	cxd5	cxd5
5	♗f4	♘c6
6	e3	e6

97

7	♗d3	♗e7
8	♘f3	0-0
9	♘e5	♘xe5
10	dxe5	

10 ♗xe5 is more solid.

10	...	♘d7
11	♕c2	g6
12	h4	

Loyal to his aggressive style, Marshall directs his efforts towards the enemy's king.

12	...	♘c5
13	h5	

13 ♗h6 is a worthy alternative.

13	...	♘xd3+
14	♕xd3	g5!

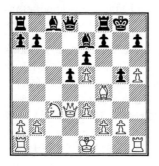

Strong defensive play. The h-file remains closed and in the absence of his light-squared bishop, White's chances to develop an attacking operation are now reduced.

15	♗g3	f5
16	exf6 e.p.	♗xf6
17	♖d1	♕b6
18	♖d2	♗d7
19	0-0	♖ac8

Intending 20...♗xc3 21 bxc3 ♗b5.

20	♖c1	♗b5
21	♕c2	♖c4
22	♕b3	♕c6
23	♖dc2	

White's strategy is questionable; why concentrate his heavy artillery on the queenside where Black is obviously stronger? A weaker player might be excused for showing a lack of understanding. In the case of Marshall, one of the best tacticians the world has ever known, it is possible that the sly fox did it on purpose – to divert his rival's attention and forces from the kingside.

23	...	♖c8
24	♕a3	♗a6

The threat ...b5-b4 seems imminent. 25 ♕d6 ♕xd6 26 ♗xd6 ♗b5! is hardly inviting.

25	b3	

Marshall assigns two exclamation marks to this move [35] and N. Minev (in *Inside Chess*) concurs. [36] But the move, which admittedly contains a most ingenious bluff, cannot save White.

25	...	♖c5?

25...♖xc3 26 ♖xc3 ♗xc3 is the first variation that springs to mind. White can play to the gallery: 27 ♖xc3 (27 ♗e5? ♗xe5 28 ♖xc6 ♖xc6) ♕xc3 28 ♕e7, when he obtains sufficient counter-chances to ensure a draw: 28...♖f8 (28...♖c6? 29 h6) 29 ♕xe6+ ♖f7 30 ♕e8+ ♖f8 31 ♕e6+ and the game ends in perpetual check.

Even better, White can play 27 ♕e7! straight away (instead of 27 ♖xc3), when he holds some advantage after 27...♕e8 (only move) 28 ♕xe8+ ♖xe8 29 ♖xc3.

We can see that the white queen's sortie causes Black a lot of trouble. Therefore the correct response is 25...♕c5! to ward off the queen's invasion while keeping all Black's trumps intact.

26 b4 ♕c6 (25...♕xb4? 27 ♕xb4 ♖xb4 26 ♘xd5) doesn't brighten the gloomy picture of White's pinned forces.

Black's actual choice. 25...♖c5, is inferior. Still, it shouldn't lose.

26	♘xd5!!	♖xc2
27	♖xc2	♕xc2
28	♘xf6+	♔f7

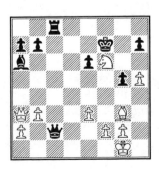

It appears as if White's burst of initiative has come to a dead end, since in addition to his material advantage Black has a double threat: 29...♔xf6 and 29...♕c1+. However, Marshall has prepared a brilliant save:

29	♕d6!!	

Once again, the motif of the combination is linked to the infiltration of the white queen on the dark squares. Once again, Black fails to realize the danger and chooses the wrong path.

29	...	♔xf6?

29...♖c7? 30 ♘g4!; or 29...♕c7 30 ♘e4! loses as well, but there is a way out – 29...♕d3! – a point missed by many commentators, who followed Marshall's annotations.

29...♕d3! 30 ♘xh7! (30 ♘e4? ♖c1+ 31 ♔h2 ♕xd6) ♕xd6 (the greedy 30...♖c1+ 31 ♔h2 ♕xh7? leads to mate after 32 ♕d7+ ♔g8 33 ♕d8+ ♔g7 34 ♗e5+ ♔h6 35 ♕xe6+) 31 ♗xd6 g4 with fair chances of holding the endgame; e.g. 32 ♗e5 ♖c5 33 ♘g5+ ♔g8 34 h6 ♗d3.

30	♗e5+	♔f5

30...♔f7 31 ♕d7+ ♔f8 32 ♗d6+ ♔g8 33 ♕xe6+ leads to the same thing. Perhaps Black underestimated the strength of White's next move:

31	f3!	1-0

A quiet, deadly move. Readers will easily find out the mate after 31...g4 32 e4+ ♔g5 33 ♕e7+.

Game 3

Almasi – Miles

Groningen 1994

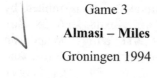

1	e4	♘c6
2	♘f3	d6
3	d4	♘f6
4	♘c3	♗g4
5	♗e2	e6

Black plays what was a rare line at the time.

6	h3	♗h5
7	d5	exd5
8	exd5	♗xf3
9	♗xf3	♘e5
10	♗e2	♗e7
11	0-0	0-0
12	a4	a6
13	♗e3	♘fd7
14	a5	

White's play is simple and logical; the d5-pawn gains him some space advantage.

14	...	♘g6
15	♖a4	♘c5
16	♖a3	

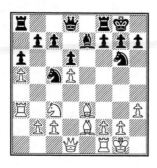

The battle has reached its first critical moment. 16...♖e8 17 b4 ♘d7 is the solid choice, leaving White with a slight pull. Black is more ambitious and opts for a line in which he activates his pieces at the cost of a pawn.

16	...	♗g5!?
17	♗xc5	dxc5
18	♘e4	♗e7
19	♖c3	♖e8

19...b6?! 20 axb6 cxb6 21 d6 ♗f6 is not as bad as it looks.

20	♗f3	

Not at once 20 ♘xc5? ♗xc5 21 ♖xc5 as 21...♕e7 forks both rook and bishop.

After the text move, a second critical moment is reached. Once again Black can select a 'conventional' line such as 20...♘e5 21 ♘xc5 ♗xc5 22 ♖xc5 ♕e7 23 ♖c3 ♖ad8, or a bolder line, which involves material concessions in return for attacking chances.

20	...	♗d6!?
21	♘xc5	♕h4
22	♘xb7	♗e5
23	♖b3	♘f4

24 g3

White must take measures against 24...♘xh3+. Almasi suggests 24 ♗g4 h5 (24...f5?! 25 ♗xf5 ♘e2+ 26 ♔h1 ♘d4 27 ♗e6+) 25 ♗d7 ♖e7 26 ♗c6 (26 ♖e1) as a better try. It is evident, however, that White must be alert, as a single error will prove fatal. 24 ♖fe1 ♗d4! 25 ♖xe8+ ♖xe8 26 ♕d2 ♗xf2+! 27 ♕xf2 ♖e1+ is one mine across the road.

24 ... ♕xh3

24...♘xh3+ 25 ♔g2 ♘f4+ 26 gxf4 ♗xf4 27 ♖h1 is insufficient.

25 d6?

This move appears very strong, as the threat 26 d7 apparently forces 25...cxd6 26 ♘xd6 ♖ad8 27 ♘xe8 ♖xd1 28 ♖xd1 with a winning advantage for White. But in 'devious chess' appearances are frequently deceptive. 25 ♖e3! (25 ♕d2 is also viable) is best, for if 25...♖ab8 26 ♖xe5 ♖xe5 27 gxf4 ♖e7 28 ♘c5 White remains unscathed.

25 ... ♖e6!!

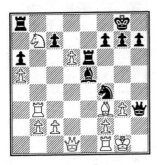

This brave and imaginative move turns the picture of the battle upside down.

26 dxc7

The natural 26 d7 is refuted by 26...♖d8! 27 ♘xd8 ♖h6 28 ♖e1 ♕h2+ 29 ♔f1 ♕h1+!. White can improve in this line with 27 ♖e1 ♖h6 28 gxf4 ♖g6+ 29 ♗g4 ♖xg4+ 30 ♕xg4 ♕xg4+ 31 ♖g3 ♕xd7 32 ♘xd8. Still, 32...♗xb2 promises Black the better ending.

26 ... ♗xc7

27 ♕d7 ♖ae8

Another fine move, intending 28...♕xf1+!, with mate to follow.

28 ♖e3 ♖xe3

29 ♕xh3 ♘xh3+

30 ♔g2 ♖xf3

0-1

Game 4

Korchnoi – Morozevich

Biel 2003

1	d4	g6
2	c4	♗g7
3	♘c3	c5
4	e3	cxd4
5	exd4	♘f6
6	♘f3	d5
7	♗g5	♘e4
8	cxd5	♘xg5
9	♘xg5	0-0?!

9...e6 10 ♗b5+! is inadvisable, but 9...♕b6, targeting d4 and b2, is a decent alternative: 10 ♘b5?! a6 11 ♖c1 0-0 is fine for Black. The text move is based on the erroneous assumption that d5 is bound to fall.

10	♕d2	♘d7
11	♗c4	♗h6
12	f4	♘f6
13	0-0	a6
14	a4	♗f5
15	a5	♖c8
16	♗b3	

"Black's play is insufficient. He is cramped and has no way of regaining the pawn"—Short. [37]

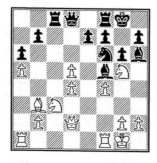

16	...	♕d6
17	♖fe1	♕b4
18	♖a3	

The white rook is temporarily misplaced, but not for long.

18	...	♖c7
19	♗a2	♕d6
20	g3	♖fc8
21	♘f3	♗f8
22	♘e5	♔g7

Black lacks a constructive plan and just waits.

23	♖b3!	

White increases his advantage. 24 ♖b6 is in the offing; 23...♘xd5? is foiled by the tactical shot 24 ♘xf7! ♔xf7 25 ♖b6!.

In this cheerless state of affairs, Morozevich brings out his fantasy and confuses the issue with some striking tactical ideas:

23	...	e6!
24	dxe6	

24 ♖b6 ♕d8 25 dxe6 seems decisive, but 25...♗c5! creates a mess. White can safely enter this line and continue 26 ♖d1 or even 26 ♘d5!? with an edge. His actual choice is also good.

24	...	♖d8!
25	♘f3?!	

25 ♘xf7 ♕xd4; but here White misses the superior 25 ♖d1! ♗xe6 26 ♖b6 (Short).

25	...	♕c6
26	♕f2	♘g4
27	♕g2	

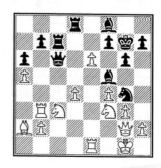

27	...	♗c5!!

An amazing concept, reminiscent of 22...♗c5! in Bronstein – Gulko. The bishop puts pressure on the g1-a7 diagonal. Accepting the offer leads to a draw: 28 dxc5 ♕xc5+ 29 ♔h1 (29 ♔f1 ♗d3+ 30 ♘e2 ♘e3+) ♘f2+ 30 ♔g1 ♘h3++.

28   ♖b6?!

The experienced Korchnoi reacts with a counter-shot. In retrospect, however, the modest 28 ♔h1! might yield better results; Black's resources seem to dry up after this.

28	...	♗xb6
29	axb6	♕xb6
30	e7	♖xd4!
31	♔h1	

31 e8=♕ ♖d2+ 32 ♔h1 ♖xg2 wins for Black. 31 e8=♘+ is tempting – it is not often that one can promotes a pawn to a third knight – but after 31...♔f8 there is strangely no win; e.g. 32 ♔h1 ♖d8 33 ♘d5 (33 h3? ♘f2+ 34 ♔h2 ♖xc3! 35 bxc3 ♗xh3 36 ♕g1 ♖xe8) ♘f2+ 34 ♔g1 ♘h3++ =.

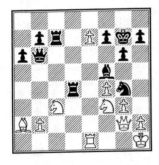

31   ...   ♖e4!!

There are times when one can hardly believe one's eyes, and this is definitely one of them. How can this work? White's e-pawn is about to graduate into an additional queen any time now... all he needs do is avert a disaster to his king... As is quite common in 'devious chess', things are fishy and unclear, to the players and observers alike.

32 ♘xe4 (32 h3? ♖xe1+ 33 ♘xe1 ♖xe7) ♖xe7 33 ♘eg5 ♖xe1+ 34 ♘xe1 ♘f2+ 35 ♔g1 ♘g4+ is a draw.

32 e8=♕(♘)+ ♖xe8 33 ♖xe8 ♘f2+ also ends in splitting the point: 34 ♔g1 ♘g4+ 35 ♔h1= (not 35 ♔f1? ♖xc3! 36 bxc3 ♕b5+ 37 c4 ♕xe8 and the tables are turned).

32   ♖xe4?

An error which should lead to a loss.

32	...	♘f2+
33	♕xf2	♕xf2
34	e8=♕	♕xf3+
35	♔g1	♗xe4?

Now the game ends peacefully. Instead, 35...♗h3! yields Black a surprising win: 36 ♕e5+ f6 37 ♕xc7+ ♔h6 with unavoidable mate on f1 or g2.

36	♕e5+	♔f8
37	♕h8+	

White is justly reluctant to enter the ending 37 ♕xe4 ♕xe4 (not 37...♖xc3? 38 ♕b4+) 38 ♘xe4 ♖c2.

37	...	♔e7
38	♕e5+	♔f8
39	♕h8+	½-½

A bizarre fight, which leaves an impression of mystery and disbelief.

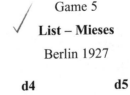

Game 5

List – Mieses

Berlin 1927

1	d4	d5
2	♘f3	♘f6

3	e3	♗f5
4	c4	c6
5	♕b3	♕b6
6	♘c3	e6
7	c5	♕c7
8	♘e5	♘bd7
9	f4	♘xe5
10	fxe5	♘e4

With this further knight exchange, the game seems to be heading towards dull equality. However, the players soon infuse it with a dose of tension by castling on opposite wings.

11	♗e2	♗e7
12	0-0	f6
13	♘xe4	♗xe4
14	exf6	gxf6
15	♗d3	f5
16	♗xe4	fxe4

The opening stage is over and Black has the somewhat better game with the open g-file inviting pressure against the white king.

17	♗d2	h5
18	♕d1!	

Removing the queen, to pave the way for the b-pawn.

18	...	♗g5
19	b4	

19	...	♕g7?

In a mutual attacking race, you can never guarantee who will be first to reach his destination. Black is preoccupied with developing his initiative on the queenside and underestimates White's chances on the opposite wing.

Leaving his king with no heavy defenders is a serious error. 19...0-0-0 was better.

20	♕e2	0-0-0
21	b5!	cxb5
22	a4	b4
23	♗xb4	♖dg8
24	♖a2	

Black was threatening 24...♗xe3+.

24	...	♖h6
25	c6	bxc6
26	♖b2	♖g6
27	♗f8?	

A flashy move, but not the best. 27 ♗a5! wins in short order. For instance, 27...♗xe3+ 28 ♔h1 ♗xd4 29 ♕a6+ ♔d7 30 ♖b7+ ♔d6 31 ♗b4+.

27   ...   ♕c7

27...♗xe3+ 28 ♔h1 (28 ♕xe3 ♖xg2+ 29 ♔h1 ♕g6 30 ♕c1 is also good) ♖xf8 29 ♕a6+ ♔d7 30 ♕b7+! (stronger than winning the queen with 30 ♖b7+) ♔d6 31 ♕b4+ ♔d7 32 ♖xf8.

28   ♖f7!

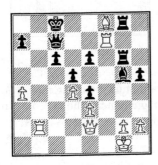

28   ...   ♕a5?

28...♕xf7! is correct. After 29 ♕a6+ ♔d7 30 ♕xa7+ (30 ♖b7+ ♔e8 31 ♖xf7 ♗xe3+ 32 ♔h1 ♔xf7 is unpromising) ♔e8 31 ♖b8+ ♗d8 32 ♖xd8+ ♔xd8 33 ♕b8+! ♔d7 34 ♕b7+, the game ends in perpetual check.

29   ♗d6!   ♗e7

The duel between the hanging bishops is amusing. Now 30 ♗xe7 (30 ♖xe7? ♖xg2+ 31 ♕xg2 ♕e1 mate) ♖xg2+ 31 ♕xg2 ♕e1+ 32 ♖f1 ♕xe3+ 33 ♔h1 ♖xg2 34 ♔xg2 ♕xd4 is unclear. However, White uncorks a decider.

30   ♖b8+   ♔d7

31   ♗b4   ♖xb8

32   ♗xa5   ♔e8

33   ♖f1   1-0

Game 6

Bellini – Pelletier

Switzerland 1999

1	e4	c5
2	♘f3	d6
3	♗b5+	♗d7
4	♗xd7+	♘xd7
5	0-0	♘gf6
6	♕e2	♖c8
7	c3	e6
8	d3	

White prefers a closed game. The alternative is 8 d4 cxd4 9 cxd4 d5 10 e5 ♘e4 11 ♘bd2.

8   ...   ♗e7

9   ♘g5!?

Embarking on some aggressive action before his army is fully deployed. The move is a bit odd but not necessarily bad.

9   ...   h6

10   ♘h3   ♕c7

11	f4	b5

12	c4

Another small surprise; one would expect White to prepare the advance d3-d4. Once again, the move chosen is completely viable.

12	...	bxc4

13	dxc4	d5

14	f5

A temporary sacrifice of a pawn, to open lines and weaken the enemy's king's position.

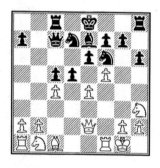

14	...	dxe4

15	fxe6	fxe6

16	♘c3

16 ♘f4 is an interesting alternative.

16	...	0-0

17	♗f4	♕c6

18	♖ad1	♖cd8

19	♘f2

White will eventually win back the e4 pawn. The resulting position will be slightly better for him due to the weakness of e6; but it might be insufficient for a full point. Therefore he preserves the tension and is in no hurry to simplify.

19	...	♘b6

20	♖xd8	♖xd8

21	b3	♗d6?!

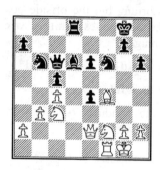

22	♗xh6!

One moment of carelessness by Black and the position explodes. The text move poses him a lot of difficult, probably insoluble problems.

22	...	♗e5

22...gxh6 23 ♘g4! is not advisable. Sample lines are 23...♘xg4 24 ♕xg4+ ♚h8 25 ♕g6; and 23...♘d7 24 ♘xh6+ ♚g7 25 ♕g4+! ♚xh6 26 ♕xe6+.

23	♘fxe4	♘xe4

24	♘xe4	♖d4

After 24...♗d4+ 25 ♚h1 gxh6, the naked black king allows White to conduct a huge attack: 26 ♕g4+ ♚h8 (26...♗g7 27 ♘f6+ ♚h8 28 ♕g6) 27 ♕g6.

25	♘g5!	♗xh2+

Both 25...♗f4 26 ♖xf4! ♖xf4 27 ♗xg7!; and 25...♗f6 26 ♖xf6! gxf6 27 ♕h5! demonstrate the destructive potential of White's attack. The rapid shift from apparent tranquility to thunder and lightning is common in 'devious chess'.

26	♔xh2	♖h4+
27	♔g1	♖xh6

The game has reached a material equilibrium, but the offside position of the ♖h6 gives White a winning advantage.

28	♖d1	♘d7
29	♕f2!	

White conducts the final stormy phase flawlessly.

29	...	♖f6
30	♕h4!	♖h6
31	♕f4	♖f6

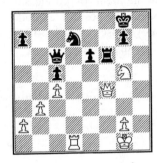

32	♕h2!	

A crafty manoeuvre which breaks all resistance. Black cannot counter White's last move with 32...♖h6? on account of 33 ♖xd7! (or 33 ♕b8+!).

32	...	♘f8
33	♖d8	

Every move contains a threat: Now Black must guard against 34 ♕h7 mate.

33	...	♖h6
34	♕b8	♖f6

Sheltering his king. But now comes a major upset:

35	♖d6!	1-0

Out of a blue sky, the black queen perishes in the middle of the board.

Game 7

Burnett – R. Bauer

Iowa 1991

1	c4	e5
2	♘c3	♘f6
3	♘f3	♘c6
4	e3	♗b4
5	♕c2	0-0
6	♘e2	♖e8
7	a3	♗f8
8	♘g3	a5
9	b3	d6
10	♗b2	h6
11	♖c1	e4!

The onset of an enterprising combination.

12	♗xf6	♕xf6
13	♘xe4	♖xe4
14	♕xe4	♗f5
15	♕d5	♕b2

The point of the previous sacrifices. The queen's sally is most embarrassing

16	♖c3	♕b1+
17	♔e2	♗e4
18	♕b5	

Unfortunately for White, he cannot simplify by returning some material

107

with 18 ♖c1, since with 18...♗xf3+!, Black wins a whole rook.

18	...	♖e8
19	♖g1	

A strange looking move but there are no useful alternatives.

19	...	♗xf3+
20	♔xf3	

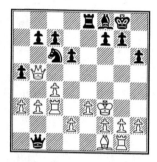

As Bauer points out, [38] here he could have crowned his beautiful combination with 20...♘d4+! 21 exd4 ♕e4+ 22 ♔g3 g5!, mating. Instead...

20	...	♕e4+
21	♔g3	♖e5?

21...♕g6+ 22 ♔f3 ♖e5 is still conclusive.

22	♗d3!	

Oops! By mere chance White is now turning the tables.

22	...	♘d4!
23	♗xe4?	

23 exd4! ♕xd4 24 ♕d7! leaves White a rook ahead, as 24...g5 25 ♕g4 and 24...♖g5+ 25 ♔f3 are both insufficient. The text move seems good enough, but...

23	...	♘e2+!

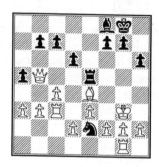

One has to reflect for a few seconds to realize that it is only a draw now. Just as 22 ♗d3 was an accidental winning move, so is 23...♘e2+ a fortuitous drawing line. This doesn't detract in any way from the resourcefulness displayed by both protagonists; on the contrary.

24	♔f3	

24 ♔g4 h5+ makes no difference.

24	...	♘xg1+
25	♔g3	♘e2+
26	♔f3	♘g1+

½-½

Game 8

Gaprindashvili – Ujtelky

Wijk aan zee II 1969

1	e4	g6
2	d4	♗g7
3	♘c3	e6?!
4	♗e3	d5
5	e5	♘e7
6	♕d2	h6?!

Before we proceed with the game, some explanatory text is required. The Czech IM Maximilian Ujtelky made a living out of bizarre formations like "the hippopotamus", consisting of placing his pawns along the third rank. Basically, Ujtelky was provoking his opponents to the extreme and was waiting for them to have a nervous breakdown. Sometimes he was slaughtered, at other times his scheme paid dividends. See for example the following position:

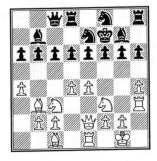

This is **Nezhmetdinov – Ujtelky**, Chigorin memorial, Sochi 1964, after 18 moves, with White to play. Nezhmetdinov obtained a won position but then freaked out, sacrificed a lot of material and went down in 75 moves.

Back to our game: Nona Gaprindashvili was the ladies world champion at the time. She played in an aggressive manner and didn't need to wait for Ujtelky to erect a third rank pawn phalanx before engaging in warfare.

7	g4	♘d7
8	0-0-0	a6
9	f4	h5
10	f5	

10	...	gxf5
11	gxh5	♖xh5

It is uncertain that White has any compensation for his pawn but that is beside the point: she is determined not to permit Black to play his kind of chess.

12	♘h3	c5
13	♖g1	♗f8
14	♕e2	♖h8
15	dxc5	♕c7
16	♘f4	♕xe5
17	♕f2	♖xh2!
18	♕xh2	♕xe3+
19	♔b1	♕xc5

Things are going well for Black; if White doesn't react swiftly, he will consolidate his material advantage.

20	♗e2	d4
21	♗h5!	

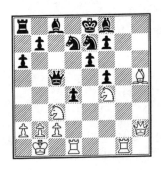

21	...	♘f6

The greedy 21...dxc3 backfires after 22 ♗xf7+! ♔xf7 23 ♕h7+ ♔e8 24 ♕h5+.

22	♘ce2	♘c6
23	♕h4	♗e7
24	♕g5	♘d8
25	♘xd4	e5
26	♘de6	

What a mess!

26	...	♗xe6
27	♘xe6	♘xe6
28	♗xf7+	♔xf7
29	♕g6+	♔f8

White has displayed a bold fighting spirit and may now claim a draw for his efforts: 30 ♕h6+ ♔f7 31 ♕g6+ and so on. Unjustifiably, Gaprindashvili goes for the full house.

30	♖h1	♘g7
31	♖h8+	♘g8

It would be nice to conclude the attack with 32 ♖g1 (32...♗f6? 33 ♕xf6+) but Black is so much ahead in material, that he can shed the queen with 32...♕xg1+! and still survive.

32	♖h7	♗f6
33	♖d7	♕c4!
34	b3	♕f1+
35	♔b2	e4+

It is now Black's turn to blossom; the white king's days are – or rather, should be – numbered.

36	♔a3	♕c1+
37	♔a4	b5+
38	♔a5	♗c3+
39	b4	♗xb4+!

40	♔xb4	♕b2+?

40...a5+, vacating a6 for the black rook, is immediately decisive: 41 ♔c5 ♕xc2+.

41	♔c5	♕xc2+?

41...♖c8+ 42 ♔b6 ♕f6+ 43 ♕xf6 ♘xf6 retains an edge.

42	♔b6	½-½

Disappointingly, Black must take the draw with 42...♕f2+ 43 ♔c6 ♕c2+.

Not the most accurate of games, but great fun, nonetheless.

Game 9

Tal – Koblentz

Riga 1960

Alexander Koblentz was Misha Tal's trainer. As part of Tal's preparation for his world-championship matches against Botvinnik in 1960 and 1961, the student and his coach played numerous training games to test some opening ideas. The present contest is one of them.

As is to be expected, the protagonists in training games do not care much about tournament-points or rating, and feel free to try out whatever comes into their minds. As you are going to see for yourselves, they did just that.

1	e4	c6
2	♘c3	d5
3	♘f3	♗g4
4	h3	♗xf3
5	gxf3!?	

This strange recapture was later employed by Tal against Botvinnik but failed to make an impression. Consequently, the idea – which does have its merits – was forgotten.

| 5 | ... | e5 |

Tal – Botvinnik (1960 match, game 3), saw the more prudent 5...e6 6 d4 ♘d7 7 ♗f4 ♗b4 8 h4 ♘gf6, when Black obtained a trusty, solid position.

| 6 | f4 | |

Tal always strove to sharpen the play. With two bishops and an open g-file, such an approach makes sense.

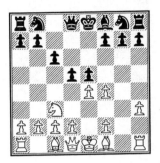

| 6 | ... | dxe4 |
| 7 | fxe5 | ♕d4! |

A good move: attacking e5, protecting e4 and restricting White's d-pawn.

8	♕e2	♕xe5
9	d4	♕xd4
10	♘xe4	♗e7
11	♗f4	♕xb2

This is not mere pawn-grabbing: by capturing the b2-pawn, the queen gains access to c3, from which it can disrupt the harmony of White's set-up.

| 12 | ♖d1 | ♘f6 |
| 13 | ♘d6+ | ♔f8 |

At the price of two pawns, White has amassed a powerful initiative; the black monarch is misplaced, his king's rook is out of play.

14 ♕c4 provides against 14...♕b4+, but after 14...♗xd6 (not 14...♘d5? 15 ♖xd5) 15 ♗xd6+ ♔g8 16 ♗a3!? ♕e5+ 17 ♗e2 ♘bd7 White doesn't have much.

14   ♕xe7+

A shocking sacrifice. Can it be sound?

14   ...   ♚xe7

15   ♘f5+   ♚e8

The only move: 15...♚f8? 16 ♖d8+ ♘e8 17 ♗d6+; and 15...♚e6? 16 ♘xg7+ ♚e7 17 ♗d6+ ♚d8 18 ♗a3+ are both disastrous.

16   ♘xg7+   ♚f8

17   ♗d6+   ♚xg7

17...♚g8 18 ♖g1 is a critical line; then, 18...h5? loses to 19 ♘xh5+ ♚h7 20 ♖g7+ ♚h6 21 ♗f4+ ♚xh5 22 ♗e2+ ♚h4 23 ♗g3+ ♚xh3 24 ♗f1 mate.

However, Black can improve with 18...♕c3+. It seems that after 19 ♖d2 ♕a1+ 20 ♖d1 ♕c3+ the game will conclude peacefully.

18   ♖g1+

18   ...   ♘g4!

18...♚h6? 19 ♗f4+ ♚h5 20 ♗e2+ ♘g4 (20...♚h4 21 ♗g5+ ♚xh3 22 ♚f1! mates) 21 ♖xg4 ♕b4+ 22 c3 ♕xf4 23 ♖xf4+ leads to approximate material equality with the black king far away from where it should be.

19   ♖xg4+   ♚f6

20   ♖f4+   ♚g7

Black elects to end this coffeehouse game in peace, rather than gamble on 20...♚g5?! 20 ♖g4+ ♚h5 22 ♗e2 ♕xc2.

21   ♖g4+   ♚f6

½-½

Game 10

Keres – T. Petrosian

Candidates tournament, Bled 1959

1	**e4**	**c5**
2	**♘f3**	**♘c6**
3	**d4**	**cxd4**
4	**♘xd4**	**g6**
5	**c4**	**♗g7**
6	**♗e3**	**♘f6**
7	**♘c3**	**♘g4**

In a Sicilian Maroczy set-up, White enjoys a space advantage. Black's last move is a familiar exchanging device.

8	**♕xg4**	**♘xd4**
9	**♕d1**	**♘e6**

The main alternative is 9...e5.

10	**♕d2**	**d6**

11	♗e2	♗d7
12	0-0	0-0
13	♖ac1	♗c6
14	♖fd1	♘c5

Winning a pawn with 14...♗xc3 15 ♕xc3 ♗xe4 turns out to be a bad bargain after 16 c5.

15	f3	a5
16	b3	♕b6
17	♘b5	♖fc8
18	♗f1	♕d8
19	♕f2	♕e8
20	♘c3	

White shuns the complications stemming from 20 ♗xc5 dxc5 21 ♕xc5 ♗b2 (21...♗h6!?) 22 ♘a7.

20	...	b6
21	♖c2	♕f8
22	♕d2	♗d7
23	♘d5	♖ab8
24	♗g5	♖e8

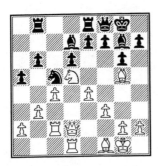

Black appears to be extremely cramped, having done nothing active so far. But odd things are about to happen...

25	♖e1	♖b7!
26	♕f2	♗c6
27	♕h4	f6
28	♗e3	e6
29	♘c3	♖d7
(30)	♗d4	f5!
31	exf5	gxf5

All of a sudden, Black's pieces have sprung to life. The queen's rook, ostensibly useless on d7, will shortly play an aggressive role on the g-file. The game was quite baffling for the commentators:

"Strange as it may appear, White, without making any obvious error, finds himself in the role of the defender" – Vasiliev. [39]

"The conventional weaknesses of the pawns d6, e6, f6, g6, actually confers flexibility on the Black position" – Keene. [40]

The game was played in an era when hedgehog formations were a rarity. But even when compared to modern games, Petrosian's strategy stands out. For instance: **Timman – Seirawan**, Reykjavik 1991: 1 ♘f3 ♘f6 2 c4 c5 3 ♘c3 e6 4 g3 b6 5 ♗g2 ♗b7 6 0-0 ♘c6 7 e3 ♗e7 8 b3 0-0 9 ♗b2 ♖c8 10 d4 cxd4 11 ♘xd4 ♕c7 12 ♘c2 a6 13 e4 ♘a7 14 ♘e3 d6 15 a4 ♘c6 16 ♖c1 ♘e5 17 ♖e1 ♖fe8 18 ♘c2 ♗f8 19 ♘d4 ♘ed7 20 ♖e3 g6 21 ♖e2 ♕b8 22 ♖b1 ♘c5 23 ♗a1 ♕a8 24 f3 ♕b8 25 ♕d2 h5 26 ♖ee1 ♔h7 27 ♗f1 ♗h6 28 ♕f2 ♘cd7 29 ♕e2 h4 30 ♗h3 ♖c5 31 b4 ♖cc8

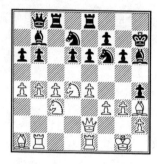

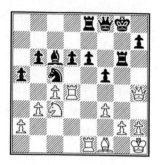

"For the fourth time in this game, a black piece returns from whence it came: ♘c6-a7-c6; ♗f8-e7-f8; ♕b8-a8-b8; and ♖c8-c5-c8. But all this manoeuvring is absolutely justified by the weaknesses White had to, or was tempted to create: a2-a4, f2-f3, b3-b4" – Soffer. [41]

32 f4 ♘h5 33 ♗g4 ♘df6 34 ♗xh5 ♘xh5 35 ♖bc1 hxg3 36 hxg3 ♘xg3 37 ♕g4 ♘h5 38 f5 ♖xc4 39 fxg6+ fxg6 40 ♘xe6 ♕c8 41 ♘g5+ ♔g8 0-1

Returning to our game: notice that Keres – unlike Timman – has not made any weakening pawn moves. Nevertheless, his position deteriorates mysteriously. The art of achieving something by doing nothing contradicts our logic, but such is 'devious chess' at times. It is only in retrospect that we realize that Black's movements to and fro were actually a well-planned, combined action.

32	♖d2	♗xd4+
33	♖xd4	♖g7

34...♗xf3 is threatened.

| 34 | ♔h1 | ♖g6 |

35	♖d2	♖d8
36	♖ed1	♖d7
37	♕f2	♕d8
38	♕e3	e5
39	f4	e4?

39...♕h4! is stronger, when an eventual ...♖h6 might be decisive.

40	♘e2	♖7g7
41	♘d4	♗d7
42	a3?	

Finally White decides to dislodge the powerful knight; however, 42 ♘b5 is stronger.

42	...	♕a8!
43	♔g1	h5
44	♖b1	

44 b4 does not bring relief: 44...axb4 45 axb4 ♘d3! 46 ♗xd3 exd3 47 ♘f3 ♕e4! 48 ♕xe4 fxe4 49 ♘g5 ♗f5.

44	...	h4
45	♖1b2	♖g4
46	♖f2	♕d8!

The influence which the black queen exerts from the back rank is remarkable.

47	b4	♖g3!!

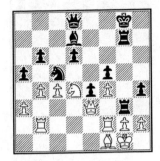

48	hxg3

Rejecting the offer will allow a black piece to land on d3 with detrimental effect.

48	...	hxg3

49	♖fd2

49 bxc5 loses to 49...♕h4 50 ♗d3 ♕h2+ 51 ♔f1 ♕h1+ 52 ♔e2 gxf2 53 ♖b1 exd3+ 54 ♕xd3 ♕xg2 55 ♖f1 ♖e7+ 56 ♔d2 ♖e1.

49	...	♕h4

50	♗e2	♖h7

51	♔f1?

A blunder. 51 ♗h5 ♖xh5 52 ♔f1 is essential, but Black retains a large advantage: 52...axb4 53 axb4 ♘d3 54 ♖xd3 ♕h1+ 55 ♕g1 exd3 56 ♖d2

♖h4 57 ♖xd3 ♖xf4+ 58 ♘f3 ♕xg1+ 59 ♔xg1 ♖xc4 and so on.

51	...	♕xf4+!

0-1

Game 11

Zaitseva – Stjazhkina

Russian women's championship, Moscow 1999

This battle is contested in 'wild west' style. Both players focus on the enemy king and look nowhere else: Were it a basketball game, the coach would run amok on the sidelines, shouting 'defence!'; but in vain.

1	♘f3	d5
2	e3	♗f5
3	c4	e6?!
4	♕b3	♘c6
5	cxd5	exd5
6	♕xb7	♘b4
7	♗b5+	♔e7

Having chosen a highly suspect opening line, Black already finds himself in major trouble.

8	♘d4	♖b8

Encouraging his opponent to capture a piece with check. Actually, after 9 ♘xf5+ ♔f6 a large part of White's advantage diminishes.

9	♕xa7

Another reasonable line is 9 ♘c6+ ♘xc6 10 ♕xc6. If 10...♖b6 11 ♕c5+ ♔e6, when White can choose

between 12 ♕c3 (12...♖xb5?
13 ♕c6+) and the fancy 12 ♗d7+!.

9	...	♖xb5

10	♘xb5

When everything appears good,
choices become difficult. 10 ♘xf5+
♚f6 11 ♘d4 is tempting, but 11...♖b6
keeps the tension, with threats like
12...♖a6 and 12...c5.

10	...	♘c2+

11	♚e2	♘xa1

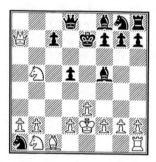

Only 11 moves have elapsed and
both sides have already forgone the
privilege of castling.

12	♘1a3	♚f6

Black's desire to remove his king
from a square on which it hinders his
other pieces is understandable.
However, 12...♚d7 gives better
chances of survival.

13	d3	♕d7

14	♗d2	♗xd3+

14...c6 15 ♕b6 is unattractive;
therefore Black decides to seek his
chances in attack.

15	♚xd3

With both kings stationed along
their respective third ranks, the
position is even more queer than the
one depicted in the former diagram.

15	...	♕f5+
16	♚e2	♕g4+
17	♚e1	♕xg2
18	♖f1	♘h6
19	♕xc7	

The game resembles checkers: Eat
(capture) as you can!

19	...	♘f5
20	♕c6+	♚g5
21	e4+	♚h4
22	exf5	♕e4+

In the final phase of the game Black
assumes the role of a wounded
animal: dangerous, but ultimately
doomed.

23	♚d1	♕f3+
24	♚c1	♗xa3
25	♘xa3	♕xf5
26	♕a4+	♚h3
27	♕f4	♖c8+
28	♚d1	♕h5+
29	f3	♚g2

While the white monarch is wandering along the first rank, Black sends his king forward, to dark alleys. Such journeys seldom end happily.

30	♕g3+	♔xf1
31	♗e3	1-0

Game 12

Tate – Ashley

New York open 1993

1	e4	c5
2	♘f3	d6
3	d4	cxd4
4	♘xd4	♘f6
5	♘c3	♘c6
6	♗g5	e6
7	♕d2	a6
8	0-0-0	h6
9	♗e3	♕c7
10	f3	♖b8
11	g4	♘e5
12	f4!?	

Deviating from the customary 12 h4, White sacrifices a pawn to accelerate the pace of his offensive.

12	...	♘exg4
13	♗g1	e5
14	♗b5+!?	

A bolt from the blue.

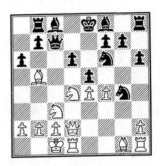

14	...	axb5
15	♘dxb5	♕d8
16	♗c5!?	

White can recoup his material investment with 16 h3 but prefers to pursue his bold attack.

16	...	d5!
17	♗a7	♖a8
18	♘xd5	♘xd5
19	♕xd5	♕xd5
20	♘c7+	♔d7
21	♘xa8	

Imaginative play has led to an extraordinary position. Black retains a material advantage but has to choose between several ways to consolidate. 21...♕xd1+ 22 ♖xd1+ ♔c6 is natural but after 23 ♖d8 ♗e6 24 f5 ♗xa2 25 ♖c8+ ♔b5 the black king is none too secure.

Black opts for another line in which he gives up some of his material gains in order to obtain a solid position.

21	...	♛d6
22	♝b8	

22 h3 is a serious alternative.

22	...	♚c6
23	♝xd6	♝xd6
24	♖d3	b5
25	♖hd1	♝c5
26	♖d8	♖xd8?!

Black is definitely the favourite in this position. However, to cash the point one needs to play precisely and Black is not up to the task. Instead of his last move, 26...♝e3+! 27 ♚b1 ♖xd8 28 ♖xd8 ♝d7 keeps a large plus. Nevertheless, the win is still there.

27	♖xd8	♝b7
28	h3	♞f2
29	fxe5	♞xh3
30	c3	♞f2
31	b4	♝e7
32	♖b8	♝g5+
33	♚c2	h5?

This loses a pawn – and a very important one – due to White's next move. 33...♞xe4 34 ♚b3 ♝xa8 35 ♖xa8 f5 is stronger.

34	a4!	♝xa8
35	axb5+	♚d7
36	♖xa8	♝f4
37	♖f8	♚e7
38	♖h8	h4
39	♖xh4	g5
40	♖h8	♝xe5
41	♖g8	f6
42	b6	

White's queenside pawns have assembled into a powerful force. A tense opposite-flanks race is about to reach its climax.

42	...	♚f7
43	♖a8	g4
44	♖a1	g3
45	♖g1	♞xe4
46	c4	♚e6
47	♚d3	f5
48	♚e3	♞g5
49	c5	f4+
50	♚d3	f3

White's chances have improved a great deal, but Black is still on top: 51 ♔e3 ♗d4+! 52 ♔xd4 f2 is useless.

51   ♖e1   f2?

51...g2! wins, e.g. 52 ♖xe5+ ♔f6 (also 52...♔xe5 53 b7 g1=♕ 54 b8=♕+ ♔f6) 53 b7 f2 54 b8=♕ f1=♕+ 55 ♔c2 (55 ♔c3 ♕a1+ with 56...♕xe5; 55 ♖e2 g1=♕ 56 ♕h8+ ♔f7 57 ♕e8+ ♔g7) 55...♕c4+ with 56...g1=♕ to follow.

In Black's defence, we must admit that the move he plays seems to win all the same...

52	♖xe5+	♔xe5
53	♔e2	♘f3
54	b7	♘d4+
55	♔f1	♘c6
56	b5	♘b8
57	c6	½-½

The continuation will be 57...♔d6 (forced; 57...♔f4? 58 ♔g2! with 59 c7) 58 ♔g2 ♔c7 59 ♔f1 and both sides cannot make progress.

An incredible position and a fitting end to this breathtaking duel.

Game 13

Larsen – Lutikov

Moscow 1959

Years go by and what was revolutionary at one time has become standard.

Bent Larsen's style created a stir among his contemporaries. He used to advance his flank pawns at an early stage, frequently with no apparent tactical reason. His strategy was very deep and well hidden: by the time his opponents realized what was going on, it was usually too late.

1	d4	f5
2	c4	♘f6
3	♘c3	d6
4	♘f3	g6
5	♗f4	♗g7
6	h4!?	♘h5
7	e3	0-0

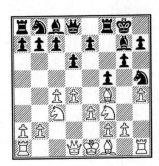

8	c5	c6

8...b6, or 8...♘xf4 9 exf4 e6 is preferable.

9	♕b3+	d5
10	g3	♘d7

11	♗e2	♛a5
12	0-0	♘df6
13	♘e5	

The opening stage is over. Black is restricted and finds it difficult to formulate a clear plan of action.

13	...	♘xf4
14	exf4	♘e4
15	♘xe4	fxe4
16	♛e3	♛c7
17	♖fc1	♗e6
18	b4	♗xe5
19	dxe5	♛d7
20	a4	♖f7
21	b5	♖d8

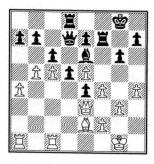

22 a5

An instructive moment. It is plain that Black's counter-chances lie in his ability to create threats with his queen and bishop. We would expect 22 ♛d4 to block the opening of any line or diagonal; but Larsen ignores his opponent's schemes, continuing with the systematic undermining of the queenside pawn-structure.

22	...	d4
23	♛xe4	♗d5

24	e6!	

24 ♛d3 (24 ♛xd4?? ♛h3) is met by 24...♛h3 25 ♗f3 ♖xf4, or even better: 24...cxb5!.

24	...	♗xe6
25	a6	♗d5
26	♛d3	cxb5?

26...bxa6 gives better chances.

27	axb7	♗xb7

Or 27...♗c4 28 ♛e4 d3 29 c6.

28	♖xa7	♛d5
29	♖xb7	♛xb7
30	c6	♛c7
31	♛xb5	♖f6
32	h5	♔g7
33	♛e5	♖dd6
34	h6+	

An echo of 25 a6.

34	...	♔f8

On 34...♔xh6, 35 g4 wins on the spot.

35	♗d3	♔e8
36	♗e4	♔f8
37	g4	d3
38	♗xd3	♛c8

39	f5	♖xd3

Or 39...♖xc6 40 ♖xc6 ♕xc6 41 g5 ♖xf5 42 ♗xf5 gxf5 43 ♕h8+ ♔f7 44 ♕xh7+ and wins.

40	g5	♖xc6
41	♕h8+	1-0

Total liquidation follows: 41...♔f7 42 ♕xh7+ ♔e8 43 ♕g8+ ♔d7 44 ♕xc8+ ♖xc8 45 ♖xc8 ♖xc8 46 h7 ♖h3 47 fxg6.

[Nowadays, advancing flank pawns has become a standard weapon in many set ups. For instance, Adams – Stohl, Nikifi/Afytos 1992, saw 1 d4 ♘f6 2 ♗g5 ♘e4 3 ♗f4 d5 4 ♘d2 ♗f5 5 e3 e6 6 ♗d3 ♘xd2 7 ♕xd2 ♗xd3 8 ♕xd3 c5 9 dxc5 ♕a5+ 10 c3 ♕xc5 11 ♘f3 ♘c6 and now White began to expand on the left wing: 12 b4 ♕b6 13 a4 ♗e7 (13...a6!) 14 a5 ♕d8 15 a6 b6 16 0-0 0-0 17 e4 ♗f6 18 ♖fd1 dxe4 19 ♕xe4 with a substantial edge for White, whose advanced a-pawn always assures him the better ending (1-0, 37 moves)].

Game 14

Murei – Malakhov

Cappelle-le-Grande 2000

The prominent attribute of this stormy clash is the multi-purpose nature of White's play. On several occasions, his moves contain, in addition to their obvious objectives, some shrewd hidden motives.

1	e4	c5
2	♘f3	d6
3	d4	cxd4
4	♘xd4	♘f6
5	♘c3	♘c6
6	♗g5	e6
7	♕d2	a6
8	0-0-0	♗e7
9	f4	♘xd4
10	♕xd4	b5
11	h4	

On the surface, the aim of this move is to mobilize the ♖h1 along the third rank, via h3. Yet another idea behind 11 h4 is to support ♗g5, thus paving the way for sacrificial lines such as 11...h6 12 ♗e2! hxg5? 13 hxg5 ♖xh1 14 ♖xh1 ♘d7 15 ♖h8+ ♘f8 (15...♗f8) 16 ♕xg7 with a terrific attack.

11	...	♗b7
12	♖h3!	♕c7
13	♗xf6	gxf6

13...♗xf6 14 ♕xd6 ♕xd6 15 ♖xd6 is advantageous for White, since 15...♗xc3 (15...b4 16 e5! ♗e7 17 ♖b6) 16 bxc3 ♗xe4 fails to 17 ♖xa6!.

14	a4!!	

An echo of 11 h4 (shades of Larsen!), this odd move (we are not expecting any activity by White on the queen's flank, after White's king has made his home there) is very deep. Shattering Black's queenside is one of its goals; it also vacates the a2 square for White's use and contests the c4 square.

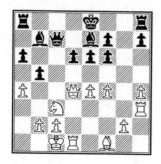

| 14 | ... | bxa4?! |

14...&c6 is more active. 15 axb5 axb5 16 &xb5 &a1+ affords Black counterplay.

| 15 | ♕xa4+ | &c6 |
| 16 | ♕c4 | |

Intending 17 ♘d5.

| 16 | ... | ♕b6 |
| 17 | f5 | &d7 |

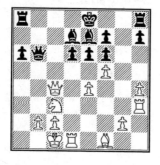

| 18 | ♕a2!! | |

A remarkable move, temporarily withdrawing the queen to a humble square. From a2 the queen threatens to increase the pressure against e6 (&c4), lends extra protection to b2 against a possible counter-attack, and more.

| 18 | ... | &f8 |
| 19 | ♔b1 | &h6 |

| 20 | fxe6 | fxe6 |
| 21 | &b5!! | |

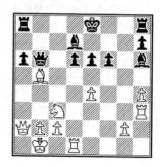

This is what we had in mind with "and more" in the previous comment. On a2 the queen pins a6, which makes White's last move playable.

| 21 | ... | ♔e7 |

Defending against 22 ♕xe6+. But once &d7 is exchanged, Black's defences crumble.

22	&xd7	♔xd7
23	♘a4	♕a7
24	e5!	fxe5
25	♕a3	&f8
26	♘c5+	♔e8

26...♔e7 27 ♘e4 doesn't bring relief.

| 27 | ♘xe6 | ♕d7 |

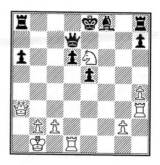

28   ♕f3!

Quickly switching his forces to mount a combined onslaught against the uncastled king. Black can only watch events.

28	...	♖c8
29	♕f6	♖g8
30	♖g3!	♕a4
31	♘c7+!	1-0

31...♖xc7 32 ♕e6+ ♔d8 33 ♖xd6+ ♗xd6 34 ♖xg8+ with mate.

Game 15

Gajewski – Trent

World Youth championship 2003

1	e4	e5
2	♘f3	♘c6
3	♗b5	♗c5
4	c3	♘f6
5	0-0	0-0
6	d4	♗b6
7	♗g5	h6
8	♗h4	d6
9	a4	

9 ♗xc6 bxc6 10 dxe5 does not achieve anything after 10...dxe5 11 ♕xd8 ♖xd8 12 ♘xe5 g5 13 ♘xc6 ♖e8.

9	...	a5
10	h3?	

A serious error; 10 ♖e1 is correct.

| 10 | ... | g5! |

11   ♘xg5

White is virtually forced into this dubious sacrifice since 11 ♗g3 ♘xe4 is plainly bad, as is 11 dxe5 dxe5 12 ♗xc6 bxc6 13 ♕xd8 ♖xd8 14 ♗g3 ♘xe4 15 ♗xe5 ♗a6.

11	...	hxg5
12	♗xg5	♔g7
13	♘d2	

13 ♗xc6 bxc6 14 f4 appears more dangerous but Black repulses White's attack with the calm 14...exd4! 15 e5 (15 cxd4 contains no threat as d4 is pinned) dxe5 16 fxe5 dxc3+ 17 ♔h1 ♕xd1 18 ♗xf6+ ♔h6 19 ♖xd1 c2.

13	...	♘e7
14	♕f3	♘h7

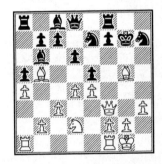

Black maintains his material advantage and his king's defences are sturdy. With correct play, he should win without trouble.

15	♗e3	♘g6
16	♘c4	♘g5
17	♕h5	♘f4
18	♗xf4	exf4
19	h4	♘xe4
20	♕f3	

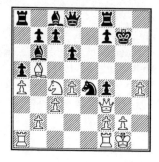

20 ... ♕xh4?!

It is hard to condemn a move which, essentially, does not spoil the win. However, the Black player was very critical of his decision, admitting that he had simply overlooked White's 22nd move. *"Any other move, protecting the knight, would have been better".* [42] Now the game becomes double-edged.

21 ♕xe4 ♖h8

22 f3

The mate is illusory. 22...♕h2+ 23 ♔f2 ♕g3+ is met by 24 ♔e2 (but not 24 ♔g1? ♖h2 25 ♖f2 ♕h4).

22 ... ♗h3!

23 ♘e3!

A tenacious defence. 23 ♕e1 (23 ♕e2 can be countered by 23...♗xg2! 24 ♕xg2+ ♔h6 25 ♗d7 ♖ag8 26 ♗g4 f5) ♕g5 24 ♖f2 ♖h6! leaves no chances, e.g. 25 ♘xb6 ♖ah8! 26 ♘c4 ♗xg2! 27 ♖xg2 ♖h1+ 28 ♔f2 ♕xg2+!.

23 ... ♕g5

24 ♘g4 f5

25 ♕e6 fxg4

26 ♕d7+ ♔h6

26...♔f8 is less convincing on account of 27 ♗c4 ♕f6 28 fxg4 ♗xd4+ 29 cxd4 ♕xd4+ 30 ♖f2 ♕xc4 and now not 31 ♖xf4+ ♕xf4 32 ♖f1

♕xf1+ 33 ♔xf1 ♗xg4! 34 ♕xg4 ♖h7; but 31 ♕f5+ ♕f7 32 ♕g5, leading to obscure complications.

27 ♖ae1 ♖ag8!

"Suddenly I was getting visions of the seemingly ridiculous king invasion..." – Trent.

28 ♖e6+ ♔h5

Not 28...♖g6 29 ♗d3!.

29 ♖e7 ♔h4

30 ♖h7+ ♔g3!

The brave king rushes forward to assist his army in the war against his counterpart.

It is not too late to ruin everything with 30...♖xh7?? 31 ♕xh7+ ♔g3 32 fxg4! and White wins.

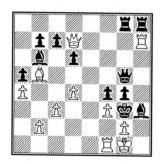

31 ♕e6

Another try is 31 gxh3 ♕g6! 32 ♖xh8? ♕c2! with mate.

31 ... ♕e5!

An effective multi-purpose move: defending against 32 ♕e1 mate, while threatening mate himself by 32...♗xd4+ 33 cxd4 ♕xd4+ 34 ♔h1 ♗xg2.

32 ♕xe5 dxe5

33 ♖xh8 ♖xh8

0-1

After 34 gxh3, 34...exd4 is lethal.

Part Four:

Assessment and Practical Tips

In the concluding part of the book we present an appraisal of the 'devious chess' phenomenon. We attempt to examine the value of this special type of chess and to assess the circumstances in which its application is particularly effective.

The final chapter addresses some practical issues, relating to the transformational process from orthodoxy to deviousness.

Chapter Ten:

Evaluating 'Devious Chess'

We have scanned enough examples to prepare ourselves for the forthcoming discussion. We now address two fundamental issues. First, we inquire whether 'devious chess' is really different from conventional chess. Assuming that it is, we'll then try to assess whether it is a worthy alternative to conventional chess.

Is 'devious chess' a different kind of chess from the game we are familiar with? I suppose that some readers will hold the view that there is nothing new under the sun. "Been there, done that, saw this" is their attitude. And anyway, what exactly do we mean by 'different'?

I gather that it is all a matter of dosage. 'A little different' is usually perceived as similar. Observing something which is 'somewhat different' induces us to search under which category to classify it. But when we witness an event which is 'significantly different', it makes us realize that we are encountering a new phenomenon.

Let us illustrate these thoughts with concrete examples. 'Normal people' and 'mentally ill people' are two opposites which, nevertheless, stand on one continuum. Normal people are sometimes a bit nervous; it happens

that they embrace a paranoid approach; they may act aggressively, be out of touch with their feelings or think in a confusing manner. Now, mentally ill persons demonstrate such behaviour and thoughts on a regular basis and in a more pronounced way. Thus it is the *frequency* and the *intensity level* of certain phenomena that make them 'different'.

We move on to a chess-related illustration. Take, for instance, an underpromotion to a knight. *[I mean a genuine underpromotion, where promoting a pawn to a queen fails]*. This is quite rare in a practical game, but not exceptional, as it does happen from time to time and I wouldn't consider this to be an attribute of unconventional chess.

Khamrakulova – Ubiennyikh

World Girls championship 2001

White to play

77 ♖d8 ♖xd8 78 cxd8=♘!

78 cxd8=♕(♖)? stalemate.

78 cxd8=♗? leaves White with the wrong coloured bishop, leading to a theoretical draw.

78...♔b8 79 ♔b6 ♔a8 80 ♘e6 1-0

Well, how about a *reciprocal knight promotion*? I'm sure this is extremely rare and has probably never occurred in a real game.

Watch how this can take shape, in the simplest of positions:

N. Kralin
6th commendation,
Shakhmaty v SSSR 1974

White to play and draw

1 c7 e1=♘+

1...e1=♕ 2 c8=♕=.

2 ♔c4 ♗g4 3 ♔b5 ♘d3 4 ♔b6 ♘e5 5 ♔b7 ♘c4 6 c8=♘! ½-½

Of course, not 6 c8=♕? ♘d6+, when Black wins.

How about the next position?

N. Elkies

Netanya Congress 1999

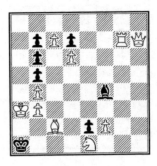

White to play and win

1 ♘d3

Black was threatening 1...♗c1 mate.

1...♗c1+!

1...e1=♕?, hoping for 2 ♘xe1 ♗c1 mate, is strongly met with 2 ♖g1!, evacuating the a1-h8 diagonal for the deadly 3 ♕h8+.

2 ♘xc1

What is Black to do now? 2...e1=♘!? has its point, since 3 c8=♕ ♘xc2+! results in stalemate. However, White foils Black's schemes with 3 c8=♖!. If then 3...♘xc2+ 4 ♖xc2, and b1 is available to the black king.

2...e1=white knight!!

Brilliant ("What's that?!" – "You heard me right!").

It appears that all White moves now end in stalemate...

3 c8=black knight!!

A mutual knight promotion; a bit unusual, though. Now, that's what I call 'different'!

Does this qualify for the unconventional chess category? Yes, absolutely.

Before we move on to assess the value of 'devious chess', we shall pause for a short philosophical digression.

Regular chess is anchored on clearly defined principles, leans on a theoretical body of research. 'Devious' chess is bizarre, risky, unstable, does not always pass the soundness test. Now we might look at them as two independent, separate entities, as presented in figure 1.

Conventional Chess   Devious Chess

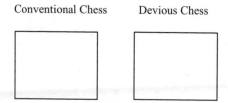

Figure 1

Alternatively, we can assume that the starting point of every chess game is identical (Fischer random chess excluded) and that on each turn, a player can choose if he'd like to stay on the conventional path, or sidestep to the 'devious' path (see figure 2).

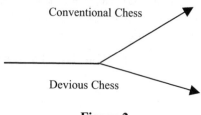

Figure 2

It is the latter view that we endorse.

The following diagram is famous; it has been reprinted on numerous occasions in chess literature.

R. Fischer – T. Petrosian
Candidates match,
Buenos Aires 1971

White to play

Black has just played 12...♕d8-d7, and White continued **13 ♖e1! ♕xa4 14 ♘xa4 ♗e6 15 ♗e3 0-0 16 ♗c5** with a considerable edge.

However, in the diagram position White can win the exchange with 13 ♗b5 axb5 14 ♕xa8. Admittedly Black obtains some sort of compensation for his material deficit but I've yet to find proof that it is sufficient. Seirawan gives 14...0-0 15 ♕a5 d4 16 ♘xb5 ♗b7 with the threat 17...♗xg2 and asserts that *"White's king is under a tremendous amount of pressure"*. [43]

'Fritz' continues 17 f3 and remains unimpressed.

Considering the availability of a second promising line, why did Fischer's 13 ♖e1 attract worldwide praise? It probably did because it leads to a safe, clear-cut advantage. All things being equal, we prefer – and justly so – the more secure path. I suppose that one shouldn't opt for 'devious chess' when ordinary means will do.

Romanishin – Jansson

Goteborg 1971

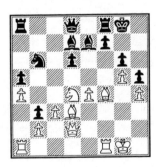

White to play

22 ♕d1?! ♘xa4 23 ♖xa4?! ♗xa4 24 ♘f5

Sparkling play by White, with more to come; but the move is hardly correct.

24...♗d7

24...d5! refutes White's play.

25 ♘h6+ ♔g7 26 ♗e3 ♗e6? 27 ♗d4+ ♔h7? 28 ♕xh5?!

28 e5! is strong (28...♗xg5 29 ♘xf7!).

28...f6?

Black can capture the queen with impunity: 28...gxh5 29 e5+ ♔g7 30 exd6+ f6 31 dxe7 ♕xe7 32 gxf6+ ♕xf6.

29 e5 f5 30 ♘xf5+! gxh5 31 ♘xe7+ ♗f5

31...♖f5 is countered brilliantly by 32 ♘xf5 d5 33 ♘h6+ ♔g7 34 ♖f7+! ♗xf7 35 e6+ ♔f8 36 ♗c5+ ♔g7 37 e7!.

32 ♘xf5 ♖xf5 33 ♗xf5+ ♔g8 34 ♗e6+ ♔h7 35 ♖f7+ 1-0

37...♔g6 38 exd6 leaves no hope.

In this instance, White preferred 'devious chess', to simple, healthy play. From the diagram position, the continuation 22 ♘xb3 ♗xa4 23 ♘d4 would have kept a steady positional plus without hair-raising complications.

In the two previous examples, 'healthy' chess clearly held more promise for the White player. But frequently a juncture separates two approximately equal roads. It is there, when one has several alternatives of more or less similar value, where the real choice lies.

1 f4 d6 2 ♘f3 g6 3 g3 ♗g7 4 ♗g2 ♘f6 5 c4 0-0 6 ♘c3 c6 7 0-0 d5 8 cxd5 cxd5 9 e3 ♘c6

White may now play 10 ♘e5, or 10 d4, both in the 'stonewall' spirit. These are the conventional chess options. However, in Basman – Tal, Hastings 1973-4, White played:

10 ♘e2 ♛d6 11 ♛a4 ♝d7 12 ♛a3!?

The queen manoeuvre leads the game to unexplored territory. In cases like this I believe that unconventional chess is roughly equivalent to conventional chess. The game was drawn in 41 moves.

S. Muhammad – Kudrin

U.S. championship 2003

White to play

Black's last move – 18...♘d5-b6 – is questionable. The scope of his queen is now reduced. White can exploit this to gain a positional edge with 19 b4 ♛f5 20 a5 ♘d5 21 c4, or 19 ♝b5 ♝xb5 20 axb5 ♛xb5 21 ♖xe7.

"I felt that White could get more with a little patience" – writes the White player. [44] Consequently he heads towards a sly, complex continuation.

19 ♝d3 ♖fe8 20 ♛e2 ♛h5?!

Black hurries to take measures against 21 ♝b5 but he may sit tight and choose 20...♝c6! 21 ♝b5 a6 (22 b4 ♝xb5).

21 a5 ♘d5 22 ♛d1!

"This quiet looking move... contains some nasty threats which my opponent failed to realize".

22...♝h6? 23 ♝e2!

The manoeuvres ♝e2-d3-e2 and ♛d2-e2-d1 are indeed baffling.

23...♛f5 24 ♛b3 ♘f4

Faced with the threat of 25 g4 (25...♛e6 26 ♝c4; 25...♛e4 26 ♝d1) and disliking the line 24...♝c6 25 c4 followed by 26 d5, Black gives up a pawn.

25 ♝xf4 ♛xf4 26 ♛xb7 (1-0, 65 moves)

Occasionally, fragments of unconventional chess are practised by stable, level-headed players, in serious competitions.

130

Zagorovsky – Rosenberg

World correspondence championship
1958 – 1961

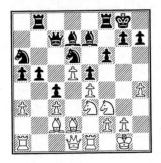

White to play

23 ♖a2?!

White feared ...a4 followed by ♘c5-b3. His last move is designed to lure his rival to another direction: *"(23 ♖a2) was played principally on psychological grounds. I wanted to make the advance ...b4 more appetizing for my opponent"* (Zagorovsky). [45]

Malakhov – Zviagintsev

5th Karpov tourney, Russia 2004

1 ♘f3 ♘f6 2 c4 g6 3 ♘c3 ♗g7 4 e4 d6 5 ♗e2 0-0 6 0-0 e5 7 d4 ♘c6 8 d5 ♘e7 9 ♘d2 a5

The game follows a well-known King's Indian line where White expands on the queenside while Black pursues his chances on the king's flank.

10 a3 ♗d7 11 b3 c6 12 ♗b2 ♕b6 13 dxc6 bxc6 14 ♘a4 ♕c7 15 c5 d5 16 ♘b6

Until now, all moves had been played before. The game Tosic – I. Sokolov, Vrnjacka Banja, 1990, saw 16...♖a7 17 ♕c2 ♗e6 18 b4 ♘d7 with an acceptable position for Black.

16...♖ad8!?

This natural move neglects the defence of his a-pawn, thus inviting White's response.

17 ♗c3! ♘xe4?! 18 ♘xe4 dxe4 19 ♗xa5

One might think that Black's 16th move had been a planned novelty, but the Black player honestly admits [46] that in his earlier calculations he had overlooked that 19...♗e6 fails against 20 ♘d5!! ♕xa5 21 ♘xe7+ ♔h8 22 ♘xc6 ♖xd1 23 ♘xa5, when White emerges with a totally won position.

Fishing in troubled waters, Black chooses to sacrifice the exchange.

19...♘f5!? 20 ♘c4

Not 20 ♘xd7?? ♕xa5.

20...♕b8 21 ♗xd8 ♖xd8

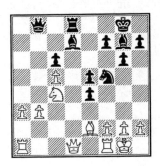

An instructive position. White is ahead in material. In addition, his queenside majority ensures him victory in any endgame. On the other hand, Black is about to plant a formidable knight on d4 and intends to push his f-pawn forward.

Objectively, White should be better; but from a practical point of view, it is easier to handle the black pieces. This is what lends this tussle its 'devious' feature: Black's chess may not be wholly sound but it presents his opponent with unusual and difficult-to-solve problems. The game is very double-edged and any result is conceivable.

22 b4?

White has many options here and this is a factor that only makes his life more complicated. The passive 22 ♕b1 ♘d4 23 ♗d1 f5 is unconvincing but 22 ♖a1-a2-d2, and 22 ♕c2 ♘d4 23 ♕xe4 ♗f5 24 ♕e3 are viable alternatives. Zviagintsev recommends yet another line, returning a pawn: 22 ♘d6 ♗e6 23 ♗c4.

22...♗e6 23 ♕e1 ♘d4 24 ♘a5 ♕c8 25 ♖d1

White underestimates the danger. 25 ♗c4 is essential, as 25...♘c2? 26 ♕xe4 ♘xa1 27 ♖xa1 is clearly in White's favour.

25...♗h6 26 ♔h1

26 ♗c4 is natural, since the continuation 26...♗g4 27 f3 exf3 28 ♕xe5 is in White's favour. Zviagintsev's analysis shows that in this case Black can force a draw with the sacrificial 26...♗xc4 27 ♘xc4 ♘f3+! 28 gxf3 ♖xd1 29 ♕xd1 ♕h3 30 ♘xe5 (30 fxe4? ♗f4 31 ♖e1 ♗xh2+ mates) ♗f4 31 ♕d8+ ♔g7 32 ♘g4 exf3 33 ♕d4+ ♔g8 34 ♘f6+ ♔f8 35 ♘xh7+ with perpetual check.

Therefore, at this stage Black may be said to be beyond any danger of losing.

26...♗f4 27 a4? ♗d5 28 ♗c4 ♘f3! 29 ♕e2

29 gxf3? ♕h3 is a helpmate.

29...♘xh2 30 ♗xd5

Evaluating the position after 20 moves, 'Fritz' emphatically prefers White. It is only here that the software shifts to preferring Black. Admittedly, 30 ♖e1 ♘f3 is no big deal either.

A typical attribute of 'devious chess' is its elusiveness. It is not easy to detect, even after painstaking analysis, what exactly had happened and where were the mistakes: White was supposed to be winning and suddenly his position is a shambles.

30...cxd5 31 f3 ♘xf1 32 ♖xf1 e3 33 c6 d4 34 ♖d1 ♗g3 35 f4 e4 36 ♘b3 d3 37 ♕xe3 ♕g4 38 ♖b1 ♕h4+ 39 ♔g1 ♕h2+ 40 ♔f1 ♕h1+ 41 ♕g1 e3!

42 ♕xh1 e2+ 43 ♔g1 d2 0-1

An aesthetically pleasing finish.

Finally, the following two episodes demonstrate unconventional chess being practiced by *both* protagonists.

Dominguez – Radjabov

World championship, Tripoli 2004

**1 e4 c5 2 ♘f3 ♘c6 3 ♘c3 ♘f6
4 ♗b5 ♕c7 5 0-0 ♘d4 6 ♖e1 a6
7 ♗f1 e5 8 ♗c4 d6 9 ♘g5**

Now *Black* can opt for the solid
9...♘e6. However, he concludes that
the threat to f7 is not as dangerous as
it looks.

9...h6

Although this may objectively be
the strongest, it is a tough decision,
since it subjects Black to a violent
offensive.

10 ♘xf7?!

...And here is a juncture where
White has to choose his path.
10 ♗xf7+ ♔e7 costs White a piece
for insufficient compensation. The
text move likewise involves a
sacrifice. However, White had at his
disposal the humble retreat 10 ♘f3 –
losing some face, admittedly – which
keeps the game in familiar channels.

10...♖h7 11 ♘d5 ♘xd5

11...♕xf7 12 ♘b6 ♕g6 13 ♘xa8
♗h3 is also playable.

12 c3

12 ♗xd5 g6 13 d3 ♘e6 is
unpromising, hence White seeks to
complicate matters.

12...♘f4!? 13 cxd4 ♗e6?

13...cxd4 14 d3 ♘e6 15 ♘xe5 dxe5
16 ♕h5 g6! 17 ♕xg6 ♕xf7 is in
Black's favour.

14 ♘xe5! dxe5 15 d5 b5?!

Later analysis suggested 15...♗f7
16 d4 ♘g6, when Black has the edge.

16 d4!

Brings total chaos to the board.
Now White gains significant counterplay and the position becomes
unclear.

**16...bxc4 17 ♗xf4 exf4 18 dxe6
0-0-0 19 d5 ♕e5 20 ♖c1 g5 21 ♖xc4
(1-0, 45 moves).**

Keres – Benitez

Olympiad, Munich 1958

**1 e4 c5 2 ♘f3 d6 3 d4 cxd4
4 ♘xd4 ♘f6 5 ♘c3 g6 6 f4 ♘c6
7 ♗c4 ♗d7 8 ♘xc6 ♗xc6 9 ♕e2**

Now Black might choose between
the solid 9...e6 or the challenging
9...♗g7 10 e5. Instead he embarks on
a breathtaking adventure.

9...d5!? 10 exd5 ♘xd5

It is now White's turn to decide if
he wants to dip his feet in hot water.
11 ♗xd5 ♗xd5 12 ♗e3 (12 ♕e5?
♗xg2) and 11 ♗e3 sidestep the main
line...

11 ♘xd5 ♗xd5

...as does 12 ♗b5+ or 12 ♗e3. But
White prefers to proceed along an
uncharted path.

12 ♕e5!? ♗xc4 13 ♕xh8 ♕d5

White has won the exchange, but Black has a strong initiative while the white queen remains far away. The game now takes a sharp turn, with enormous complications.

14 ♔f2 f6 15 ♗e3?!

15 ♕xh7! is better for White, for instance: 15...♕f5 16 ♖e1 ♕xc2+ 17 ♔g1 ♗d5 18 ♕h3.

15...♕h5 16 ♖he1 ♔f7 17 ♗d4 e5

17...♖e8! is much better.

18 fxe5 ♕h4+ 19 ♔g1 ♕xd4+ 20 ♔h1 ♕h4 21 ♖e3 ♖e8 22 ♖h3

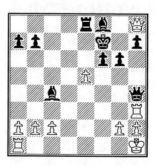

22...♕xh3 23 ♕xf6+ ♔g8 24 gxh3 ♗d5+ 25 ♔g1 ♗c5+ 26 ♔f1 ♖f8 27 ♕xf8+ ♔xf8 28 ♖d1 ♗c6 29 a3 a5 30 ♔e2 ♔e7 and the game was **drawn** on the 42nd move.

Chapter Eleven:

Becoming an Unconventional Player

Where to Find 'Devious Chess' Material?

When chess players seek to find model games to emulate, they are usually games that are played in top tournaments by leading grandmasters. But if you are on the lookout for models of 'devious chess', you'd probably be wise to look elsewhere: super-grandmasters playing in super-tournaments are likely to practise a solid, conventional type of game.

In the process of gathering material for this book I discovered hidden treasures in offbeat magazines and on obscure web sites, run by average club-players.

Games played on the internet are also a major reservoir of 'devious chess'. Computer-games are another source of interest, since software is committed neither to conventions nor to theoretical fashions – it simply scans the best moves. Here, for example, is a contest between two software programs, playing with their opening books closed.

✓ Fritz 7 – Hiarcs 7.32
2001

The game is lifted from the site of Southbourne Chess Club, [47] which takes an active interest in computer chess. The time limit for each player was 25 minutes for the game + 5 seconds per move.

1 e4 e5 2 ♘c3 ♘f6 3 ♘f3 ♘c6 4 ♗c4 ♘xe4 5 0-0?! ♘xc3 6 dxc3 ♕f6 7 ♘g5 ♘d8 8 f4 b5 9 ♗d3 h6 10 ♘h7

10 ♘e4 sticks to normal paths (10...♕b6+ 11 ♔h1 d5). The text move is a side step and immediately crosses a point of no return, since from h7 the knight is unable to participate in the future battle.

10...♗c5+ 11 ♔h1 ♕h4 12 fxe5 ♗b7 13 b4 ♗f2 14 ♗xb5 c6 15 ♗d3 ♗g3 16 h3 c5 17 ♗f5 ♘e6 18 bxc5 ♗xe5 19 ♕d3 0-0-0 20 ♖b1 ♘xc5 21 ♕e3 ♗d6 22 ♖b4 ♕e7 23 ♕g1

The whole game gives an impression of being contested between two beginners. Yet if you follow its moves with the aid of your computer, you'll find that most of them are simply the strongest.

23...g6 24 ♖e1 ♞e6 (25) ♖xb7 ♝c5 26 ♝a3

I suspect one is unlikely to find similar positions in the games of Kramnik, Anand or Leko. Nor is this type of a game likely to be included in the latest *yearbook*.

26...♔xb7 27 ♝xe6 fxe6 (28) ♝xc5 d6 29 ♝xa7 ♖xh7 30 ♖b1+ ♔a8 (31) ♝b6 ♖b8 32 ♖b4 ♖b7 33 ♕f1 ♔b8 34 ♕a6 ♕e8 35 a4 ♖he7 (36) a5 g5 37 ♝a7+ ♔c8 (38) c4 ♖ec7 39 c5 dxc5 40 ♝xc5 e5 41 ♖b6 ♔d7 42 ♖xb7 ♖xb7 43 ♕xb7+ ♔e6 44 a6 1-0

Another method of unearthing 'devious chess' treasures is to look out for games of specific players. Tal, Shirov, Morozevich, Murey, Miles, Rossolimo, Larsen, Bronstein and Planinc, among others, frequently produce(d) startling ideas.

Kudishevich – Kagansky

Tel-Aviv 2002

1 e4 c6 2 ♞c3 d5 3 f4 dxe4 4 ♞xe4 ♞f6 5 ♞f2 ♝f5 6 g4

6...♝e6 7 h3 g6 8 ♞f3 ♝g7 9 ♝g2 ♕c7 10 d4 ♞a6 11 0-0 (1-0, 34 moves).

Sutovsky – Morozevich

4NCL, England 2004

1 e4 c5 2 ♞f3 ♞c6 3 ♝b5 ♞f6 4 e5 ♞d5 5 0-0 a6 6 ♝xc6 dxc6 7 ♞g5!? ♕c7 8 c4 ♞b4 9 a3 ♞d3 10 ♞xf7

10...♖g8!? (11) ♕f3 ♕d7 12 ♞d6+ exd6 13 ♕xd3 dxe5? (13...♕f5!) 14 ♕xh7 ♕f7 15 ♖e1 (1-0, 32 moves).

It is tempting to go through the following game, if only because of the names of both protagonists.

Kavalek – Tolush

Polanica Zdroi 1964

1 d4 ♘f6 2 c4 e6 3 ♘c3 ♗b4 4 e3 c5 5 ♘f3 0-0 6 ♗d3 d5 7 0-0 b6 8 a3 cxd4 9 axb4 dxc3 10 bxc3 dxc4 11 ♗xc4 ♕c7 12 ♕b3 ♗b7 13 ♗e2 ♘bd7 14 ♗b2 ♘g4

The standard play up to here suddenly flares up with this move. Black starts to position his pieces in the proximity of the enemy king, provoking and creating threats at the same time.

15 g3 ♘df6 16 c4 ♘e4 17 ♘d4!

A strong counter-stroke. 17...♘d2 18 ♕c2 (18 ♕c3 is also good) ♘xf1 19 ♗xg4 is clearly to White's advantage.

17...♘gf6 18 ♕c2 ♘g5 19 f3 ♕e5

Black has placed all his eggs in one basket: his pieces occupy offensive outposts; yet if they fail to deliver, he will find himself in a lost position. The battle had reached its climax.

20 e4 ♘fxe4

As planned...

21 fxe4 ♗xe4

With the double threat 22...♘h3 mate and 22...♗xc2 but White's calculation is more precise.

22 ♘f3! ♘h3+ 23 ♔g2 ♕f5 24 ♕c3 f6 25 ♖ad1 (1-0, 34 moves).

Isolated fragments of 'devious chess' may be found everywhere. Hard to believe, the following melee stems from a correspondence tourney.

Schatzle – Filartiga

Correspondence, Argentina 1974

1 e4 c5 2 ♘f3 e6 3 d4 cxd4 4 ♘xd4 ♘f6 5 ♘c3 ♗b4 6 e5 ♘e4 7 ♕g4 ♕a5 8 ♕xg7 ♗xc3+ 9 bxc3 ♕xc3+ 10 ♔e2 b6 11 ♕xh8+ ♔e7 12 ♗a3+ ♕xa3 13 ♕xc8 ♕b2 14 ♘b3 ♘c6 15 ♕xa8 ♕xc2+ 16 ♔e3 ♕xf2+ 17 ♔xe4 ♘xe5

Black threatens 18...d5+ 19 ♔xe5 ♕e3 mate. 18 ♔xe5 ♕e3+ 19 ♕e4 d6 (f6) mate doesn't help. However, White has so much superfluous material, that sacrificing a whole queen for the sake of providing a flight square for his king turns out to be good enough for victory.

18 ♕f8+! ♔xf8 19 ♔xe5 ♕e3+

If 19...♔e7 20 ♔e4 and the king escapes to a safe haven.

20 ♔d6 ♔e8 21 ♔c7 1-0

Black resigned, assuming that in the long run White's material advantage will prevail.

How to Become
a 'Devious Chess' Player

Actually, you don't have to do much. The board and pieces are the same, the rules of the game remain intact. What is needed is a change of attitude, a more carefree approach; to stop worrying about rating points; to have less fear about losing. A player who replaces the task-oriented goal of winning with the spirit of adventure and fun can produce glimpses of 'devious chess' in no time. This change may be achieved by everyone, whatever his level or age.

Ossip Bernstein (1882-1962) was one of the strongest players in the world of his day. Always a chess amateur, he possessed a daring, risky and adventurous style. Here is a sample, lifted from the "excavations" of Swiss IM and chess historian Richard Forster.

O.Bernstein – Flamberg
Vilna 1912

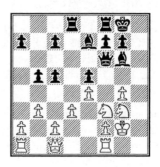

White to play

18 ♖h1

Transferring his big guns against the black king's position.

18...♕e6 19 ♘f5 c4 20 ♕g1! f6 21 ♘3h4 ♗h7 22 ♕h2

With the idea to counter 22...cxd3 by 23 ♘g6!.

22...♔f7 23 dxc4 bxc4 24 ♕g3 ♗c5 25 g5

This should have been the beginning of the end. Black is helpless.

25...♗xf5 26 ♘xf5 fxg5

27 g6+ was threatened, *inter alia*.

27 ♖h7 ♖d2

Now the simple 28 ♖f1 would have won shortly (28...♖g8 29 ♕xg5 eyeing g7 and d2). Instead—

28 ♖xg7+?! ♔e8 29 ♖xc7?

Probably expecting 29...♖xf2+? 30 ♕xf2 ♗xf2 31 ♘g7+, but missing Black's obvious resource:

29...♖xf5 30 exf5 ♕d5+ 31 ♔h3 ♖xf2

A drastic turn of events. 32 ♖d1!! is a computer move which still keeps the upper hand, e.g. 32...♕xd1 33 ♕xe5+ ♔d8 34 ♖c8+! ♔xc8 35 ♕xc5+ with 36 ♕xf2; or 32...g4+ 33 ♕xg4 ♖f3+ 34 ♔h4 ♗f2+ 35 ♔g5! (clearer than 35 ♔h5 ♖xf5+!) ♕xd1 36 ♖c8+ ♔e7 37 f6+. Bernstein opts to return the exchange.

32 ♖xc5 ♕xc5 33 ♕xg5 ♖f3+ 34 ♔g4 ♕d5

After the earlier misfortune, most players would deliver a perpetual check here, conceding a draw. Not Bernstein.

35 ♕g6+ ♔e7 36 ♕h7+ ♔f8 37 ♕h6+ ♔e7 38 ♖e1 ♖c3 39 ♕g7+ ♔d8 40 ♕f6+ ♔d7

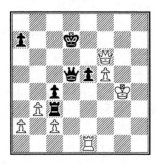

41 ♔h4!

In view of the open position, this quiet move is very brave—avoiding a lethal check on g2 and evacuating the g-file for the use of his rook.

41...♕d4+?

Black was given room for error and he falls for it. 41...♖xc2 is correct and safe.

42 ♔h5 ♕d5

After 42...♖h3+ 43 ♔g6 ♕g4+ 44 ♔f7 ♖h7+ 45 ♔f8 it is the black monarch who is in trouble.

43 ♕g7+ ♔d8 44 ♖g1!

"Showing nerves of steel"—says Forster. Bernstein continues to retain maximum tension.

44...♖h3+ 45 ♔g6 ♔e8

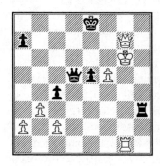

46 ♕c7!!

Switching the offensive to the left wing. White had the hindsight to understand that the advanced position of his king is a virtue, not a liability.

46...♕g8+ 47 ♔f6 ♕f8+

The tactical point of his 46th move is that 47...♕xg1 (47...♖h6+ 48 ♖g6) allows mate in one.

48 ♔e6 ♖h6+ 49 ♔d5 cxb3

The ending after 49...♕f7+ 50 ♕xf7+ leaves Black with no chances.

50 ♖g7! 1-0

I found an intriguing suggestion of Kenny Harman on the chesscafe.com forum; Mr. Harman proposed converting to what he called Zen Chess: *"I believe we have made chess into some computerized monster whereas chess is as simple as breathing... There is a great deal to be unlearned... it is possible to play freshly and spontaneously... Chess then is not about winning or losing but about self-realization."* [48]

The concept of unlearning, mentioned above, is quite instructive. The thing is that during many years of learning the game, we clutter our mind with a lot of useless, even damaging sort of material. Dr. E. Lasker once stated that it took him many years to forget what he had been taught about chess as a youngster. Unlearning made him stronger – testified the ex-world-champion.

Some years ago there appeared a book by Kostyev, entitled *From beginner to expert in 40 lessons*. [49] We still await a complementary volume entitled "From a knowledge-able player to a novice in 40 lessons".

What to Expect?

Becoming a 'devious' player may feel strange, as does almost any serious change we introduce to our life. Initially, results may fall short and the whole idea may appear foolhardy. If you aspire to be a candidate for the world chess championship, resorting to 'devious chess' is probably a wrong idea.

But if being a fairly strong club player is good enough for you, then in the long run, you can look forward to many chess adventures and fascinating complications you didn't even think were possible... like the following episode:

Plaskett – Short

Plovdiv 1984

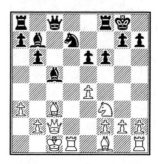

White to play

14 b4!?

A committal move, weakening his king's defences.

14...♗e7

14...♗xf2? loses to 15 ♔b2 ♗e3 16 ♕d3, with a decisive double attack.

15 ♕b3 ♖f7

15...♗xe4 16 ♗c4 is another possible line. Plaskett suggested 16 ♕xe6+ ♔h8 17 ♔b2 but Black bounces back advantageously with 17...♘c5! 18 ♕xc8 ♘a4+.

16 ♗c4 ♘f8 17 ♘d4

Now 17...♗xe4 18 ♘xe6 b5 19 ♗xb5 ♘xe6 (19...♕xe6? 20 ♗c4) 20 ♗c4 ♗f5 (20...♘g5 21 h4; 20...♘d8 21 ♖he1) 21 ♖he1 a5! 22 ♔b2 is to White's advantage, according to Plaskett. [50]

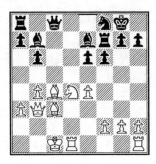

17...♗xb4!

A startling tactic. The bishop is sacrificed to enable the ♖f7 to shift to the c-file.

18 axb4

18 ♕xb4 a5! 19 ♕b3 (19 ♕b5 ♗a6) ♖c7.

18...♖c7 19 ♘xe6 ♖xc4 20 ♘c5!

The quick transformation from a standard position to a storming tactical volcano is amazing.

20...b5

20...♗a6 might be better, e.g. 21 ♖d4 bxc5 22 ♖xc4 ♗xc4 23 ♕xc4+ ♕e6, with approximate equality.

21 ♖d4 ♔h8 22 ♖xc4 bxc4 23 ♕xc4 a5 24 ♖d1 axb4 25 ♕xb4 ♗c6

White is a pawn up, but the position is still messy (**1-0**, 42 moves).

Solutions to Puzzles

Page 26

Tzesarsky – Ma. Tseitlin:

37...♖d3+ 38 ♔c2 ♕d2+ 39 ♔b1 ♕xb2+! 40 ♖xb2 ♖d1+ 0-1

Page 34

Moor – Jenni

17 ♗d5 dxc3 18 bxc3 ♘a5 is unappealing. 17 c4, or 17 ♕f3 is adequate.

17 ♗c2?

Missing Black's concealed intention, White loses.

17...♗c8! 18 f3 dxc3 19 bxc3 ♘d4! 0-1

Page 48

Short – Sulava

10 ♗c7

Closing the noose.

10...♘a6 11 a3 ♕xc3 12 ♕xc3 ♘xc7 13 ♘f4

Strangely, White forgot to convert his material advantage into victory and the game was drawn in 59 moves.

Pages 64-65

1) 10 ♗g5! ♗xf3 11 ♕c1!! 1-0

Black prepared to answer 11 ♕d2 with 11...♗b4!. By side-stepping this mine the game is suddenly over, for if 11...♗b4+ 12 ♔f1 ♕xd4 then 13 ♕c8 mate.

2) After the calm **19...♗f6!** (what was an error a move ago, is now correct), White's attack is repelled and he suffers more material losses:

20 ♕h4 ♗xb2 21 ♘e7+ ♔g7 0-1.

3) **25 ♖b7 ♗xc5 26 ♕xc5 ♖f7!** Seemingly turning the tables... **27 ♕a5!!** but it doesn't...

The game concluded **27...♕e8 28 ♖xf7 ♕xf7 29 ♕d8+ ♕g8 30 ♕xg8+ ♔xg8 31 f4** and **1-0** on the 39th move.

4) 25...♕c4

Threatens both 26...♕e2 mate and ♖xd4. 26 ♕f2 is strongly countered by 26...fxe5 or 26...c5!, ready to meet 27 b3? with 27...♖xd4! 28 ♖xh7+ ♔g8

26 ♕f3 ♖xd4 27 ♘xg5

Do you fancy White's position now?

27...♖h4!

Protects h7, attacks h1, and prepares to answer 28 ♖xh4 with 28...♕xh4+ followed by 29...♕xg5.

28 ♖h3 ♔g8!?

Renewing the attack on g5. 28...♖xh3 29 ♘xh3 ♕h4+ 30 ♘f2 ♖e8 31 ♖d2 ♖xe5+ 32 ♔d1 is unclear. [20]

29 exf6

Is White on top?

29...♖e8+ 30 ♔d2

But not 30 ♔f2? ♕c5+.

After the text move, the apparently strong 30...♖d4+ 31 ♔c1 ♖xd1+ 32 ♕xd1 ♕f4+ 33 ♔b1 ♕xg5 actually loses to 34 f7+ ♔xf7 35 ♕d7+; but Black has another trump:

30...♖e2+

Surely this is the end for White, isn't it?

31 ♕xe2 ♕xe2+ 32 ♔c1

Hey, what's going on? Having just won White's queen, Black is forced to surrender his own (32...♕e8 33 f7+).

32...♕xd1+ 33 ♔xd1 ♖xh3 34 gxh3 ♗c8 35 f7+ ♔g7 36 ♘xh7 ♔xf7 37 ♘g5+ ♔g6 38 h4 ♔h5

White retains a slight advantage, which proved insufficient and the game was **drawn** on the 60th move.

Pages 72-73

1) 14...♖xh2 is a blunder.

15 ♖xh2 ♕g1+ 16 ♗f1! ♕xh2 17 ♕xd5!!

Winning material.

17...exd5 18 ♘f6+ ♔e7 19 ♘g4+ ♔e6 20 ♘xh2 dxe5 21 ♗e2 f6 22 ♗d2 ♗d6 23 0-0-0 e4 24 ♖h1 d4 25 ♘g4 e3 26 ♗a5 ♗f4 27 ♘xf6! 1-0

2) *"My opponent thought that I erred"* – says the Black player. [26] White was counting on 42...hxg6 43 ♕xh6, or 42...♗xd2 43 ♘xe7+.

42...♗xh3!! 43 ♘xe7+ ♖xe7

Not only must White return material (44 ♕xh6? ♘g4+), but g4 is now irrevocably weak.

44 ♕e2 ♗xf1 45 ♖xf1 ♘g4+ 46 ♔g1 f5 47 ♕f3

Or 47 ♗xf5 ♖xe2 48 ♗xc8 ♗e3+.

47...fxe4 48 dxe4 a3 49 ♗a1 ♗g7 and **Black won** shortly.

3) **17...♘xd2**

18 ♔b2!!

A quiet move which regains material with interest.

18...♗a6 19 ♗xa8 ♘c4+ 20 bxc4 ♖xa8

Black seeks refuge in an opposite-coloured bishop ending, but in vain.

21 c5 ♖b8+ 22 ♔a1 ♕g6 23 ♖d1 ♖e8 24 ♕a4 ♖f8 25 c6 ♗e2 26 ♖d2 ♗g4 27 c7 ♗e6 28 ♖d8 f5 29 ♕c6 ♔f7 30 ♖xf8+ (1-0, 35 moves)

4) 2 ♖g4? ♘e2+!!

A rare appearance of a 'Novotny' theme in a practical game: 3 ♖xe2 blocks the bishop, thus enabling 3...♗xg4; 3 ♗xe2 blocks ♖e1, and falls short to 3...♕xe3+ with 4...fxg4. Black won.

5) In the game, Black responded to **1 ♖fxf6?** with **1...♖xd6?** and remained a pawn down after 2 ♖xd6.

Instead, he should have played **1...♕xf6! 2 ♕xd7** (forced: 2 ♖xf6? ♖d1 mate; 2 ♖xd7? ♕a1+) **2...♖e7!! 3 ♕d8** (3 ♖xf6 ♖xd7 and the mate threat costs White his rook) **3...♖xe4!** when White's back rank weakness is fatal (4 ♖d1 ♕xd8, or 4 fxe4 ♕f1 mate).

Page 94

Castro – Geller

Both 21...♗f8 and 21...♘f4 are strong and keep Black's advantage. In the game Black chose **21...bxc4? 22 ♗xc4 ♘a5** (22...♖b8 23 ♕g3 ♖d8 24 ♕b3=), probably missing **23 ♕b6!**

Here Black could have opted for the secure 23...♘c6 24 ♕b3 ♘a5=. But he was still trying for the full point. After further inaccuracies he lost as follows:

23...♕xb6 24 ♗xb6 ♘xc4 25 ♗xd8 ♘f4 26 b3 ♘e5 27 ♖d6 ♘e6 28 ♗a5 ♘c5 29 b4 ♘e4 30 ♖xa6 ♘d3 31 ♔f1 ♗d4? 32 ♖a8+ ♔g7 33 ♖d8 1-0

References

1 *Soviet Chess 1917 – 1991* / A. Soltis / McFarland, USA 2000 / p.69-70

2 *My Best Games* / Y. Geller / (in Russian) / p. 96-99

3 *Fire on Board* / A. Shirov / Cadogan 1997 / p. 116 – 118

4 E. Gufeld / in *Makedonsky Schach* 1/1972 / p. 33

5 *Soviet Chess* / N. Grekov / Capricorn Books, New York 1962 / p.116-117

6 *Twic* (the week in chess) web site / February 2003 / Reported by Rod McShane

7 B. Harley / in "The Gambit Club" / in *Chess Monthly* 12/1994 / p. 20

8 *The South African Chessplayer* 10/1964 / p. 155-156

9 Hack Attack / in *Kingpin* N. 17-18, 1991 / p. 37-38

10 *Chess Secrets I learned from the Masters* / Ed. Lasker / Hollis & Carter, London 1952 / p.256-263

11 Genrich Chepukaities / Interview on web site "Russian Chess"

12 *200 Open Games* / D. Bronstein / Dover Publications, New York 1973 / p. 231

13 *Startling Castling* / Robert Timmer / Batsford 1997

14 J. Roycroft / in *Chess Monthly* 6/1996 / p. 45

15 *The End of Illusions* / Computer Analysis of U. Ballas / "Schahmat" (Hebrew) 6/1997 / p. 23-24

16 *The Magic of Chess Tactics* / D. Mayer & K. Muller / Russell Enterprises, USA 2002 / p. 103-107

17 U. Avner / *Schahmat* 3/1969 (Hebrew) / p. 67

18 M. Czerniak / *64 Squares* (Hebrew) 1957 / p. 136

19 *Attack with Michail Tal* / Cadogan 1994 / p. 1

20 *The Chess Analyst* / Jon Edwards / Thinker's Press, Devenport 1998 / p. 84-89

21 *Secrets of Chess Intuition* / A. Beliavsky & A. Mikhalchishin / Gambit, 2002 / p. 31

22 *Modern Chess Miniatures* / N. McDonald / Cadogan 1995 / p. 63-64

23 Y. Geller / in *Chess* 10/1975 / p. 13-14

24 G. Kasparov / in *New in Chess* 10/1995 / p. 46-53

25 Winning by Blundering /A. Avni / in *Kingpin* N. 28, Spring 1998 / p. 39-41

26 Israel U-20 championship 1999 / in *Schahmat* 12/1999 / p. 16-17

27 *The World Champions Teach Chess* / Y. Estrin & I. Romanov (ed.) / A&C Black, London 1988 / p. 105

28 V. Salov / in *New in Chess* 1/1992 / p. 34-35

29 *Emanuel Lasker, the Life of a Chess Master* / J. Hannak / Dover, New York 1991 / p. 64

30 L. Kavalek / in *The Washington Post* 5 July 2004 / p. C10

31 *The Test of Time* / G. Kasparov / Pergamon Press 1986 / p. 106

32 T. Karolyi / in *Kingpin* N. 16, winter 1990 / p. 12

33 Botvinnik – Petrosian / in Russian periodicals, analysis by M. Tal. Hebrew translation in *Schahmat* 5-6/1963 .

34 Gulko in *Shakhmaty vs. SSSR*, and Sovietsky Sports

35 F. Marshall / *Marshall's best Games of Chess* / Dover, 1960

36 N. Minev / *Inside Chess* 5/1999 / p. 25-26

37 N. Short / *The Daily Telegraph* 10/8/2003

38 R. Bauer / in web site: www.jeremysilman.com

39 *Tigran Petrosian, His Life and Games* / V. L. Vasiliev / Batsford, 1974 / p. 94-96

40 Raymond Keene / *Learn from the Grandmasters* / Batsford, 1998 / p. 92

41 R. Soffer / in *Schahmat* (Hebrew) 7/1994 / p. 27

42 L. Trent / in www.essexchess.org.uk

43 Y. Seirawan / in *Learn from the Grandmasters* / Batsford, 1998 / p. 152

44 S. Muhammad / in www.thechessdrum.net

45 V. Zagorovsky / in *Chess Mail* 1/2003 / p. 24-25

46 V. Zviagintsev / in *New in Chess* 3/2004 / p. 59-61

47 www.geocities.com/southbourne_computers

48 www.chesscafe.com – Bulletin Board

49 A. Kostyev / *From Beginner to Expert in 40 Lessons* / Collier Books, 1984

50 J. Plaskett / in *Kingpin* No. 10 / p. 18-21